Haiku

—the sacred art

Haiku
—the sacred art

A Spiritual Practice
in Three Lines

Margaret D. McGee

Walking Together, Finding the Way®
SKYLIGHT PATHS®
PUBLISHING

Haiku—The Sacred Art:
A Spiritual Practice in Three Lines

2009 Quality Paperback Edition
© 2009 by Margaret D. McGee

Library of Congress Cataloging-in-Publication Data
McGee, Margaret D.
Haiku— the sacred art : a spiritual practice in three lines / Margaret D. McGee.
   p. cm. — (The art of spiritual living)
Includes bibliographical references and index.
ISBN-13: 978-1-59473-269-0 (quality pbk.)
ISBN-10: 1-59473-269-8 (quality pbk.)
   1. Haiku—Authorship. 2. Spiritual life—Prayers and devotions. I. Title.
PN1525.M34 2009
808.81'41—dc22

2009034690

Manufactured in the United States of America

Cover Design: Jenny Buono
Cover Art: Hummingbird © Pavel Bortel—Fotolia.com;
Leaves © Dra Schwartz—iStockphoto.com

SkyLight Paths Publishing is creating a place where people of different spiritual traditions come together for challenge and inspiration, a place where we can help each other understand the mystery that lies at the heart of our existence.

SkyLight Paths sees both believers and seekers as a community that increasingly transcends traditional boundaries of religion and denomination—people wanting to learn from each other, *walking together, finding the way.*

SkyLight Paths, "Walking Together, Finding the Way," and colophon are trademarks of LongHill Partners, Inc., registered in the U.S. Patent and Trademark Office.

Walking Together, Finding the Way®
Published by SkyLight Paths Publishing
An Imprint of Turner Publishing Company
4507 Charlotte Avenue, Suite 100
Nashville, TN 37209
Tel: (615) 255-2665
www.skylightpaths.com

CONTENTS

INTRODUCTION

shown a flower
a small baby
opens its mouth
                    —Seifu-ni (1731–1814)

I wrote my first haiku when I was forty-five years old, in a beginner's poetry-writing class. Nowadays, it is common for haiku to be taught in elementary and middle schools, but that was not the case when I was a child. Though I had a brief encounter with haiku in a Japanese literature class during college, I did not know much about the form, and until four other novice poets and I came together for our first class, I had never tried writing haiku myself.

We met at our teacher Carol Light's home, a small cabin that already seemed pretty full with her rambunctious young golden retriever. We all found a place to sit, and once Rover had thoroughly expressed his joy at our arrival and settled down, the class got under way.

To start us out, Carol introduced the idea of an *image*—a picture in the mind's eye. Then, to tone up our observation and description muscles, she set us down with some exercises. Soon I was happily studying a spray of pink flowers in a vase, jotting down every descriptive word or phrase that came to me. I noted the color, shape, and parts of the flowers, the arch of the branch, the clusters of tiny mauve leaves. A single spray of flowers is a remarkably complex object, once you take the time to really look.

As the minutes passed, I saw more and more. Finally, my sheet of paper full, I ran out of things to record. If this spray of flowers had more to tell, I'd have to hear it from other members of the class. Incredibly, one of them was still writing. Carol said she'd give us another minute to finish up. After such concentrated work, I was happy to rest.

As I sat back in my chair, a flicker of light and movement on the surface of the vase caught my eye. I leaned forward, and the flicker moved with me. Suddenly my focus changed, and I found myself gazing deep into the rounded surface of the flower's container. The vase's smooth glaze, acting as a curved mirror, reflected back the room and everything in it, with me in its center. The reflection had been right in front of me all the time, without my ever noticing.

> a shift in focus—
> the whole room reflected
> in a flower's vase
> —M.D.M.

For a moment, time stood still. Then I grabbed my pencil and managed a few more quick notes before Carol called a halt to this part of the session.

What happened during that moment when time stood still? In the thinking part of my mind, nothing much happened at all. Today my mind easily makes a connection between the flower, the vase, and all of God's creation. I think about how my attention is usually drawn away by one thing after another—some beautiful, others not so beautiful. Life's little details consume my thoughts and distract me from this different way of seeing, a way that shows all of creation contained and reflected in each individual part of creation. Including me. I think about how I can look, and look, and see so much and still not see the whole, until a change in focus makes me sit up straight, revealing the truth of what's been right in front of me all along.

But at that particular moment, I wasn't thinking at all. I was completely taken up in *feelings*—a mixture of surprise, delight, even awe. For a flash of time, I felt the underlying unity of all things. Then the moment passed, and I started writing again.

I didn't know it, but I was having a "haiku moment"—a moment when the mind stops and the heart moves.

After the exercise, Carol introduced us to haiku. We read examples from the Japanese masters, and she described the form as it's usually written in English: a short three-line poem that conveys feeling through imagery, rather than through abstract ideas or opinions. We read examples that were structured in three lines of five, seven, and five syllables, and we read others that were shorter and less formally structured. Then she set us out to write some haiku from the material we had generated in our exercises.

From the beginning, I loved writing haiku. I quickly bonded to writing verse in this ordered way. I'd dabbled in poetry before, but always felt inadequate to the task. Trying to write poetry with meter, I ended up producing convoluted phrases that did not say what I meant to say. Adding rhyme only made it worse. But when I abandoned meter and rhyme to try to write free verse, the result was no better. Without a structure, I had no idea where to end my lines and usually broke them off wherever it looked good to me on the page. A little instruction would

> haiku moment: a moment when the mind stops and the heart moves

have helped, but then the fear factor kicked in. Intimidated by "real poets" and afraid to be the most clueless person in the room, I steered clear of poetry-writing classes.

It took years for me to wake up to the idea that being clueless was nowhere near the problem it had seemed. In fact, when it comes to learning something new, cluelessness turns out to be the perfect and only place to start. So if you have come to this book curious about writing haiku but uncertain about your own poetic experience or abilities, take heart. You are exactly where you need to be, and you have just the tools you need to begin writing haiku as part of your spiritual practice.

> When it comes to learning something new, cluelessness turns out to be the perfect and only place to start.

That night in Carol's class, I wrote my first haiku and had fun doing it. Mysteriously, I don't have these haiku anymore. Working on this introduction, I dug through my files and found the one marked "Carol Light's Poetry Class." It contains the course syllabus, instructions for exercises, and the poems I wrote from later exercises. But for some reason, it contains none of the haiku from that first night. I can't find them anywhere. This is odd, because I'm a packrat about my own writing. I still have yellowed, handwritten short stories from elementary school.

So, I wrote the above poem, "a shift in focus," today while remembering my haiku moment. The memory brought the image to mind, and with the image came a return of surprise, delight, and awe.

To remember the moment but lose the poem is oddly appropriate in a book about writing haiku. In haiku, it is the moment, not the poem, that really matters.

Examples in This Book

Over centuries of a long and illustrious tradition of Japanese poetry, haiku emerged as a distinct form of verse with well-established conventions. As the form continues to develop and evolve in Japan and around the world, its definition has been the source of much lively discussion. Examples in this book include poems that adhere closely to the conventions of the classical haiku form, as well as many that take a more freewheeling approach. (For more about the history and conventions of the haiku form, see chapter 3, "A Companionable Form.")

For haiku written and published in the West, conventions in matters such as capitalization, punctuation, and syllable count have evolved quite a bit since the form was first translated into English in the latter years of the nineteenth century. You will see a wide range of styles represented in this book.

When I took Carol's class, she advised us not to let the syllable count take control. Brevity is the heart and soul of haiku, and she suggested that if we found ourselves tempted to add a syllable for no better reason than to get to seventeen, we should resist the temptation.

I heard her advice, but did not take it to heart, at least not at first. I liked pressing up against the 5-7-5 syllable form. Fitting my words into that simple structure helped me tighten and polish the imagery without getting all tied up in knots. At the same time, the form provided a plausible reason to end one line, start another, and finally end the poem. It made me feel competent. Heck, I knew what a syllable was, and I could count up to five, and seven, and five again! Yet, over the years since taking Carol's class, I have found myself

> In haiku, it is the moment, not the poem, that really matters.

paying more attention to the moment at hand in writing my haiku, and less attention to the number of syllables in a line, finally embracing Carol's advice about not letting the 5-7-5 form make the poem longer than it needs to be.

As I continue to play with and expand my haiku experience, I enjoy trying new techniques, reading haiku by different writers, and sharing haiku experiments with others. More recently, I have begun writing verses in response to passages from scripture, and I now lead workshops on the technique. These workshops remain one of my favorite ways to write haiku. Starting with a passage from scripture or sacred poetry, we write individual poems, and we also pass words and themes from the passage around the circle, creating group poems of linked verse. Each person's response to the passage is unique, rising out of that person's matchless life and spirit. In the linked verse, both our individuality and our deep communion find voice. Some of the examples you'll see in this book were written in those workshops. A few are the first haiku—or even the first poem—that some people have ever written.

Brevity is the heart and soul of haiku.

When I launched my website, In the Courtyard, at www.inthecourtyard.com, I decided to include a page for haiku. Each month I post a brief passage from scripture or other sacred text and invite readers to send their haiku responses, which I then post with the passage. I receive verses from friends, from people who've taken my workshops, and from far-flung web pilgrims who happen upon the page and like the practice. Some examples in this book are from people who have posted their haiku on my website.

Thanks to the generosity of accomplished poets and translators, this book also includes a broad range of examples written by haiku poets of the past and present. In my hometown, I have been blessed to find the Port Townsend Haiku Club, where I have met able poets who, in their devotion to the craft, show just what goes into writing well-made, moving, and transformative haiku. You'll find some of their work represented in these pages. I've also included a number of my own haiku that illustrate how haiku has become part of my spiritual practice.

The haiku form developed in Japan, where Shinto and Buddhism are the two major religions. While I am a Christian, and my own practice is grounded in the Episcopal Church, I have seen that writing haiku touches a human longing that lies deep within all great faith traditions: the need to find our place in the world, to feel in our hearts our relationship to each other and to all of creation. Writing haiku is compatible with any approach for a deeper inner life, and for that reason, this book contains examples drawn from a variety of faith traditions— including the time-honored tradition of taking a long walk and paying attention.

> Unchurched, still I turn
> when the meadowlark
> begins to sing
> —CARL MAYFIELD

If you practice within a faith tradition, I hope you find examples here that you can use within the context of your faith, as well as examples from other traditions that illuminate the common path we all take together. For those outside traditional religious community, I hope the examples from faith traditions will bring the depth of the centuries to your personal spiritual practice.

Practices in This Book

At the end of each chapter, you will find suggestions for ways to make the practice of writing haiku part of your spiritual life. Many of the practices can be completed by yourself; others are specifically designed as group activities. Even if you've never written a poem before, you can undertake these practices and have fun doing them, either on your own or with others.

As you enter this book, and begin or extend your own haiku practice, the images and connections that come out of your imagination will be expressions of your creative self, showing that you are made in the image of the Spirit

Capturing moments of deep feeling that make you feel alive and whole—moments that make you aware of holiness—is a way to relate to the Creative Spirit through the "now" of *this* moment.

that creates all things. Capturing moments of deep feeling that make you feel alive and whole—moments that make you aware of holiness—is a way to relate to the Creative Spirit through the "now" of *this* moment, just as it is. In writing and sharing your haiku, I hope you will experience a deepening relationship with the Spirit as it lives and breathes in the world, in those around you, and in you.

CHAPTER ONE

The Heart of a Moment

the distant mountain
reflected in his eyes ...
dragonfly
     —Kobayashi Issa (1762–1826)

A haiku expresses the heart of a moment in a few brief lines. Using images and senses, a haiku brings feeling to life.

A haiku is a form of instant communion. A haiku involves an exchange of sensory experience: taste and touch, bread and wine. In haiku, the experience is shared in a few brief words, offering both the feeling of the moment and the insight that we are not alone.

Mysteriously, words that evoke deep feelings are usually not about emotions or big ideas. Instead, they are most often about the world around us: physical things that can be seen, touched, tasted, smelled, or heard. To carry its feeling across time, a haiku offers not the idea of an experience, but the experience itself.

> Then God said, "Let there be light"; and there was light.
> And God saw that the light was good.
>   —GENESIS 1:3–4A

When the Creative Spirit speaks, things come into being: light, sky, earth, seas, plants, the sun and the moon, all living creatures, and time itself. A haiku speaks in the language of creation: the language of images and senses, of the natural world, of things as they are. Writing a haiku is a way to *re-create* the essence of a moment and allow it to touch our hearts anew. In this way, we become a conduit for the Creative Spirit—listening, feeling, responding, and passing on the mystery of life.

Alive in the Moment

Although I did not start writing haiku until my middle years, I did discover the joy of recording life's moments and feelings at a young age. It happened when my high school English teacher, Mr. Edler, gave us an assignment to hand in every Friday at least one paragraph about our lives during the previous week. He called it "keeping a journal."

> A haiku speaks in the language of creation.

I had tried diary writing before without ever managing to complete a whole month, let alone a whole year. But right away this journal writing felt different, and the difference sprang from having an audience. Mr. Edler returned our entries with an occasional note written in the margin—a comment, a question, or encouragement to write more. Suddenly, my observations and internal musings actually had meaning outside my own hormone-addled brain. Within a few weeks, I was taking paper and pencil with me wherever I went. By the end of the ten-week term, my journal was nearly one hundred pages long and my life as a writer had changed for good.

> new pond—
> the first tadpole
> wriggles over clean stones
> —CHRISTOPHER HEROLD

When I revisited the pages of this journal recently, an entry from February 1968 caught my attention:

I have been told that being young is "special." I hope not, because I never want to lose what I have now.

I look at the sky, and blue or gray or white—it's beautiful. Then I look down at where the horizon meets the sky, and even though it has different colors and shapes, the earth has the same beauty. People and cats and cement and chairs and food and business suits and white hose and everything. They're all the *same*. Do you understand? *[Note: This was 1968, and just about every girl I knew owned at least one pair of white hose.]*

But there are other times when everything is ugly and dingy and old. Walking to town along the railroad tracks, I look down at the movie theatre and the five-and-dime, and all the stores are shaped in grotesque and ridiculous forms. It is like a tiny fantasy world of gnomes and distorted fairies.

And then I am depressed and everything is very bad. It's not like that all the time, but it is sometimes.

So when they tell me that being young is "special," does that mean that when I grow up only beautiful things will be beautiful and only ugly things will be ugly? Does it mean that I will reach a norm in how I feel, so that sometimes I may feel a little better or worse, but there will never be ecstasy or hell?

Hell is no fun, but it is good for thinking. I can think best when I am in hell.

I read those words with mixed feelings and a twist of the heart. On the one hand, young Margaret's qualms about the future are on target, or nearly on target: the highs and lows have evened out. Though ecstasy and hell have not completely disappeared, they now come more often in glimpses and moments, almost never in the endless drowning waves of youth. What she was afraid of losing has been nearly lost.

Yet I do not want to go back. I am happy to be off the roller coaster of youth. I am grateful to be trundling along in my well-used but fairly reliable station wagon of middle age. I want to tell young Margaret that it is not so bad to grow up, and that even fleeting glimpses of heaven and hell carry great and lasting gifts, and that you do not have to be depressed in order to think interesting thoughts.

What I *do* want back—the loss that twists my heart—is her youthful ability to be engaged in life, moment to moment, in a way that hardly feels possible anymore.

> A haiku is ... a hand beckoning, a door half-opened, a mirror wiped clean. It is a way of returning to nature, to our moon nature, our cherry blossom nature, our falling leaf nature, in short, to our Buddha nature.
>
> —R. H. BLYTH

I want the experience of being alive in this moment, and I want to know I am having it. The breeze on my skin. Air moving in and out of my lungs. Light in the trees. The songs of birds. A human touch, skin to skin. I want these things because I know now, after more than a half century of living, that in these simple, ordinary moment-to-moments, the Sacred comes out to play. It is in the air, the light, and the song that heaven makes a home. To have the experience of this moment, and to know I'm having it, is to be alive with the One who made the moment.

To have the experience of this moment, and to know I'm having it, is to be alive with the One who made the moment.

While I was busy growing up, something in me fought against that kind of life. Even today, something wants to mask the moment, soften its edges, turn aside. Over the years, that something has grown adept at getting what it wants. Now I find myself stuck with habits of inattention that must be faced down simply to *have* this moment of life.

For example, I like to eat food with lively flavors, so that's the kind of food I cook for myself. Then, as often as not, I read a book or magazine through the meal, diverting my attention from the savor of the moment. At the end of lunch, I can hardly say what I ate or how it tasted. Wise people advise me to stop reading while I eat and pay attention to my food. So I do that and appreciate the benefits, for a while. Then I find myself reading at mealtime again. What can I say? I like to read while I eat!

One way to have the experience of life in this moment, and to know you're having it, is to write it down.

Lately, I have been trying this approach: read a paragraph, then stop reading, take a bite, look up, and focus on my taste buds. Look around the room and out the window. Chew, swallow, then look down, and read another paragraph. Repeat until final paragraph, or until plate is empty. I have not yet mastered the technique, but it shows promise.

Ignoring the food I love is only one example among many distractions I throw between me and the moment—all the while longing for engagement in life.

How do I break through the shell of years to experience the essence of life today? I consult the expert: young Margaret and her high school journal. Reading those words written long ago, I feel again the pain and joy of young life. What is more, I can tell how these feelings are carried to me across the decades because they are evoked by particular words on the page. They ride along with the cats, cement, chairs, food, business suits, and white hose. They come out of the storefronts in a tired old Midwestern town, seen from a rise and imagined as a fantasy world of gnomes and distorted fairies. It is in those images and senses, noted and written down long ago, that life moves across time and distance to touch my heart today. As a result, I have the experience of being alive, and I know it.

One way to have the experience of life in this moment, and to know you're having it, is to write it down—its physical truth—as simply and directly as you can. Write it down not for your eyes alone, but to be shared.

> Writing haiku offers the chance to honor, hold, and fully experience a fleeting moment that takes you out of yourself.

You might write it down to share the moment with a friend, or with any other person who is open to entering into the feelings of the moment with you.

Your audience might be *you* at an unknown future date—older, changed in some ways and just the same in others, but still glad to remember this moment and share its life again.

Or your audience might be the Creative Spirit itself, the One who makes both you and each moment.

In short, you could write a haiku. And trust me, you can. Even if you have never written a poem in your life, you can write a haiku. Haiku writing is like low-tech instant messaging: it's in the "now," easy to share with others, and a great way to practice saying more with less.

A Shock of Recognition

Writing haiku offers the chance to honor, hold, and fully experience a fleeting moment that takes you out of yourself, a moment that hints at the deeper unity that lies beneath the surface of things. Such a moment inspired this haiku by Christopher Herold, a lay monk who practices Buddhism, and founder of the haiku journal *The Heron's Nest*.

> dragonfly ...
> a stream of thought pauses
> on the stone Buddha
> —CHRISTOPHER HEROLD

Here is how Christopher describes his haiku moment:

> I was sitting on a bench in a Japanese garden. There were a lot of dragonflies around and my "monkey mind" was every bit as busy as they were. All of a sudden, one big dragonfly whizzed past my right ear, stopped, turned around, and then hovered no more than three or four inches from my nose, staring straight into me. It was so startling that my thoughts stopped abruptly; my attention was entirely focused on the dragonfly. It didn't occur to me that I'd stopped daydreaming until a moment later when the dragonfly zipped over to the stone Buddha and alighted on his shoulder. It was then that I realized that my thoughts were no longer wandering. And it was then, at that very moment of recognition, I began to think again. In the timeless moment just before, however, the dragonfly was more than a dragonfly. I saw it for what it had been all along: Buddha. And at that same instant, so was I.

Christopher's moment of recognition came in a face-to-face meeting with a dragonfly. In contrast, the inspiration for this next poem by Brad Offutt occurred in a moment of recognition with a homeless man at a shelter.

> He has no home, yet
> cleans his boots until they shine—
> mirroring my soul.
> —BRAD OFFUTT

Brad is a member of St. Paul's Episcopal Church in Port Townsend, Washington, my home parish. St. Paul's is one of many churches in the community that provides volunteers to fix meals and monitor the homeless shelter located in the basement of the American Legion Hall. One night when Brad was serving as monitor at the shelter, he saw one of the homeless men quietly shining his boots, and in observing that quiet action, had a moment of recognition.

> Watching a man who has so little spend so much care on his boots, and sensing the air of comfort around him, I got it in a flash that we are so much alike. Never thought of it before, but Jesus and the twelve [disciples] must have taken good care of their sandals too. That they were homeless radicals does not mean they were scruffy! Sometimes I think that [the] shelter is the best place to see God Among Us!

The images in Christopher's and Brad's haiku reflect what was happening in the world around them at a particular moment. An image can also rise from the inner world of imagination. That's where I found the girl for my "open-air café" haiku.

> open-air café …
> a girl in torn black tights
> sends text
>   —M.D.M.

I had been reading my high school journal and remembering those white hose that everybody wore back in the late sixties. Suddenly I had a strong mental image of a teenage girl today. In my mind's eye, she was sitting at a table in a public place, such as an open-air café. She was dressed all in black, from an onyx nose ring to black tights with a hole in one knee. She picked up a cell phone from the table in front of her and started to click.

The girl appeared clear and sharp in my mind's eye, and yet I had never "met" her. She was drawn from any number of teenagers I have walked by and sat near in airports, food courts, and coffee shops. At those moments, I probably would have said that the black-clad young women with their piercings and cell phones did not have much in common with me—if I thought about them at all. My haiku moment occurred when memory and imagination came together, connecting white hose to black tights, relating my young self writing in her journal to a different young woman, forty years later, texting on her phone. In that moment, I had a lot in common with every twenty-first-century teenager. In a flash, deep down, we are the same.

We human beings are carriers of meaning. That's one of the ingredients we add to the mix of the cosmos—a sense of relationship between one thing and another. We love to connect the dots, and we use our brains to do it, figuring out how to make fire, navigate the seas, and communicate with each other instantly around the world. Every now and then, the connection comes not from the figuring brain, but straight from the heart. With a shock of recognition, we feel the bond between our deepest place and the world outside.

> Every now and then, the connection comes not from the figuring brain, but straight from the heart.

Writing a haiku is one way to honor this moment and pass it on.

Here and Gone

A haiku takes us down to the bones of a moment. Those bones are unique to that particular moment, just as our structural bones are unique to each of us and our individual DNA.

At the same time, every moment is already passing away—here and gone—just as our bones, too, will someday be no more than dust and ashes.

> You are dust, and to dust you shall return.
> —GENESIS 3:19B

> For the present form of this world is passing away.
> —1 CORINTHIANS 7:31B

These two ideas—the unique, underlying essence that makes each thing and moment like itself and nothing else, along with its fleeting transience—are basic to Buddhist thought and the Hindu Upanishads. They are also central to the early development of haiku in Japan and the basic principles in the art of writing haiku today. As the poet-translator Patricia Donegan puts it, "Haiku brings us the birth and death of each moment."

A great haiku can hold in its few lines both the truth of this moment today, and the truth of how things pass away. This often-quoted poem by the early master of haiku, Matsuo Bashō, is a good example.

> summer grasses—
> all that remains
> of warriors' dreams
>   —MATSUO BASHŌ (1644–1694)

Bashō wrote this haiku after visiting the site of a historic incident that occurred in the aftermath of an epic battle fought hundreds of years before he was born. His haiku records in the simplest terms what was left at a location that had once contained a bridge and a castle: summer grasses, which themselves would wither away by year's end. The poem makes the connection between the present moment, even now passing away, and the dreams of those who fought and died at that same spot long ago.

A haiku takes us down to the bones of a moment.

A haiku expresses the heart of a moment in a few brief lines. At the core of every moment lies the heart of the cosmos, and my heart, and yours. In *The Haiku Handbook,* William J. Higginson says that "haiku not only give us moments from the writer's experience, but go on to give us moments of our own. The central act of haiku is letting an object or event touch us, and then sharing it with another." In this communion, we partake and share in the heart of life.

Practice: Now and Then

Earlier in this chapter, I said that a haiku "offers not the idea of an experience, but the experience itself." How is that possible?

It is possible through *images*—pictures in the mind's eye—rather than through explanations. Often a haiku contains two related images. For example, the haiku by Issa at the start of this chapter contains the image of a distant mountain and the image of a dragonfly.

> the distant mountain
> reflected in his eyes ...
> dragonfly
> —Kobayashi Issa (1762–1826)

Issa does not try to explain why he put these images together in one poem or how they are related. As a result, the relationship unfolds in our imaginations, and we have the chance to enter into the moment with him and share in its experience.

In this Now and Then practice, you will develop a list of images, then put two of them together to make a haiku. Images that evoke complex feelings often touch more than one sense (sight, sound, smell, taste, and touch), as well as other aspects of consciousness, such as the sense of balance and the sense of movement. This practice is designed to help you be fully present to all your senses and develop mindfulness in the moment at hand.

You will need paper and pencil, and at least twenty minutes of quiet time. Give yourself the time you need.

(This practice works as well in a group as it does individually. If you are doing this practice in a group, you will want additional time to share your results with each other. Throughout the practices in this book, I have included in italic parentheses tips for writing and sharing haiku in groups.)

- First, look over the whole practice; then go through the steps one by one.
- Start with a grid using these seven headings: **Scent, Taste, Sound, Touch, Balance, Movement,** and **Sight.** You can either use the grid below or draw your own on a fresh piece of paper, leaving room under each heading for a sentence or two. Allow some extra room under **Sight.**

Scent	Taste
Sound	Touch
Balance (in or out of balance)	Sight
Movement (moving or still)	

- If it is practical, go outside and find a place to sit comfortably. If that's not practical, get comfortable where you are.
- Relax, breathe, and look around. Start with the first heading, **Scent.** Can you smell anything right now? Or do you see something that has a scent—maybe a lavender in bloom? (Or even a pile of dog poop!) Write down the first thing you notice with a distinct scent. Do not spend much time describing the smell; let the image do the work. For example, "Rover's old pillow" carries a scent that needs no description.

- Now close your eyes, relax, and let your mind wander. Go back in memory, focusing on your sense of smell. Let the memory of a particular scent come to you, possibly something from childhood, or something from last week. For example, one scent image from my memory is "campfire wienie roast." Open your eyes and, under the **Scent** heading, jot down a few words that evoke the scent from your memory.

- If no memory comes in a moment or two, that's okay. Instead of jotting down a scent memory, just look around right now and jot down, under the heading for **Sight,** the first thing you notice.

- Repeat the process for each heading, including an immediate sense and one from your memory. When you come to **Balance,** look for something in this moment that feels to you either *in balance* or *out of balance.* Then look for the same kind of dynamic in your memory. When you come to **Movement,** look for something that is either *moving* or particularly *still.* Some of your images may evoke more than one sense and fit under more than one category. You may also have many entries under **Sight,** and that is okay.

- Once you have an image or two under each category, stop and look them over. *(If you are doing this practice in a group, this would be a good time to share images among the group. If you have the means, write the headings where everyone can see them. Under each heading, write down two or three images from those who are comfortable sharing.)*

- Now that you have a number of images full of sensory feeling, it is time to make connections. On a fresh sheet of paper, write down two images from your list that resonate with each other. You can choose two images that rise up and appeal to you right now. They may come from the present moment or from your memory. They may come from the same sense category or from different categories. You may have a distinct idea of how they are related, or you may only sense a relationship between them.

- Condense one of the images down to a single short phrase. Find the essence of the image and include only what's needed.
- Condense the second image down to its essentials in a longer phrase or sentence, still including only what's needed.
- Put your two images together in a three-line haiku. Make the shorter image either the first or the last line, and spread the longer image over the other two lines.

Tip 1: If you find yourself obsessing over the placement of commas, dashes, or semicolons, try eliminating all punctuation marks and let the images themselves do the work. Then add only the punctuation you really need.

Tip 2: If you are accustomed to writing haiku with a 5-7-5 syllable count, feel free to use that form in your haiku. Or, if you are new to haiku writing, you may want to give that approach a try. Your shorter image will contain five syllables, and your longer image will contain twelve, broken into two lines of seven and five syllables. Just be careful not to let counting syllables take over the experience of the moment. Give yourself permission to pay more attention to the image than to the number of syllables in a line.

- Finished? Take a moment to enjoy what you've written. Congratulations on your haiku! *(If you are doing this exercise in a group, give all the group members a chance to share their haiku if they choose. For tips on reading haiku aloud in a group, see the sidebar on page 23.)*

Mindfulness has been called a state of calm awareness in the moment. How did noting and jotting down your sensory impressions change your awareness of each passing moment? Did you find the practice calming, inspiring, or both?

In the coming week, you may want to delve into the images from this practice to write more haiku. You can also repeat the practice anytime and anywhere you have twenty minutes or so to reconnect with all your senses.

Tips for having a good experience when writing and sharing haiku in a group:

- After completing an exercise, give all the group members a chance to share their haiku if they choose. Appoint someone to keep an eye on the clock, so that anyone who wants to share has time to be heard.
- When you read your haiku out loud to others for the first time, don't rush the words. In Japan, it is traditional when reading haiku aloud to say the poem twice, and this practice is especially helpful in a group setting when your haiku is being heard for the first time. Read your poem once slowly, wait a moment, then read it a second time.
- As a listener, it's your job to simply be present with an open heart and hear what's offered. When a haiku touches you deeply, you might share, in a positive context, how it affects you.
- Unless the poet asks for suggestions, or the group has been purposely set up as a writer's critique group, this is not the time to offer critical feedback.

CHAPTER TWO

A Simple Prayer

Never more alone
the eagle, than now surrounded
by screaming crows
                    —James W. Hackett

On a late afternoon in December, my thoughts a confusion of fluttering and squawking fears, I set out on a long walk down the country roads near my home. The fears had to do with a building project that was about to begin on my home property. After months of talk and planning, it was time to break ground for my studio, a small stand-alone building where—in theory, at least—I would be able to focus without the distractions of working at home. (I am not much of a housekeeper, but when the writing is not going well, even swabbing out a toilet takes on a strange and compelling attraction.)

We had found a couple of expert shed builders to put up the shell, and a variety of local contractors to insulate, wire, and finish the one-room structure. Now it was time to schedule the work and start writing checks, and my feet were cold as ice. Although my husband, David, supported the project, he politely declined to take on the role of general contractor. This was my baby, the labor mine to bear.

Intensely aware of my inexperience in the building trade, I feared making bad decisions that would result in expensive mistakes. I imagined doubtful or confused contractors asking, "Really? Is that *really* what you want?" I pictured their carefully courteous expressions as I dithered about decision after decision.

Or—and the more I thought about it, the more likely this seemed—I was afraid of truly spectacular failure. What if I ended up stuck in a brand new studio where I still couldn't write? Those toilets would be only a few hundred feet away. What would stop me from trekking back and forth between the studio and the house, and finding even more distractions in my weedy garden? Time, effort, and resources all wasted.

> I wanted to remember and record the moment…. I also wanted to give myself a path back to that feeling.

Failure! Even worse—admitting failure! Snippets of future awkward conversations clamored through my brain: apologies to David for wasting our money, explanations to family and friends about why my new studio had reverted to its roots and turned into an extra-fancy storage shed. With these black crows circling and screaming in my mind, I wondered if I should just abandon the studio and the writing life with it. Could it possibly be worth the pain and risk?

A much quieter voice from my heart suggested that I not give my fears and self-doubts too much weight in this matter. I knew other women writers and artists who had work spaces outside their homes, for reasons that were similar to mine. Some of them had encouraged me to take the plunge. Maybe their perspective was better than mine. This seemed like a real possibility, since in times past I had chosen what seemed to be the safer road, only to find that it did not lead anywhere I wanted to go. In retrospect, I might have gone to more interesting places if I could have put fear aside and made the leap of faith.

In the midst of doubt, I knew I wanted the kind of life that grew out of greater faith. And yet a fog of indecision still clouded my mind. Though I tried to soar free, my fears would not be shaken off.

So I took a walk. I placed one foot in front of the other and chewed on fear and hope. My path took me alongside drab winter fields and past a wooded lot with horses standing among the trees. I walked by lanky roadside wild rhododendrons, their buds small and tight for midwinter, and dirt driveways that curved back into woods, and huge old cedars that had been standing in place long before I was born.

Become a spectator in the greatest drama ever played—the drama of the opening leaf, the rising bread dough, the drilling woodpecker, the chasing dog, the cloud that crosses the moon.

After forty minutes or so, long enough for my muscles to loosen and my gait to become fluid and easy, long enough for thoughts and memories to come and go, the road took a turn.

After being enclosed in woods, suddenly I looked out over a wide, overgrown meadow. It was dusk. In the draining light, every color blended into soft grays and browns. Two ghostly deer stood in the middle of the meadow. Stopped by this unexpected gift of beauty, I paused for a moment to watch them. Then, magically, a dark mound just beside the pair—a mound I had taken at first sight for a big clump of weeds—moved and took on shape. Raising her head from the broken winter grasses, the third deer turned to look right at me.

> a turn in the road
> two—no—three deer emerge
> from the dusk
>
> —M.D.M.

Suddenly, I felt that things would be all right. Success seemed a little more likely, and failure, if it came, less dreadful. My heart lifted. The feeling was one of unexpected gifts that wait around a turn in the road, of new circumstances that contain more possibility than first seen. The feeling rose up inside me, but I cannot say that it originated with me alone. Mysteriously, this sense of grace emerged along with the discovery of the third deer.

> Haiku is a way of letting God know that we are paying attention.

As my walk circled back toward home, I began to compose in my mind the haiku "a turn in the road." I wanted to remember and record the moment when my heart lifted. I also wanted to give myself a path back to that feeling when moments of doubt and fear returned.

That evening I called the excavating contractor and got myself on his schedule. The studio was mine to make happen. And although rocky places lay on the path ahead, I never regretted taking on the role of my own general contractor. Today, I write these words in my studio, where I work every day. At times it is still a struggle to focus, but I have written many words here in the past four years, and I am not tempted to run home and swab out the toilets instead.

> For you shall be in league with the stones of the field, and
> the wild animals shall be at peace with you.
>
> —JOB 5:23

One of the best ways for me to find peace and a sense of belonging in the world is to *look out into the world*. Wrench my attention away from the inward thoughts, fears, and dramas that consume so much of the conscious mind, step outside, and look around. Become a spectator in the greatest drama ever played—the drama of the opening leaf, the rising bread dough, the drilling woodpecker, the chasing dog, the cloud that crosses the moon. Then, in a few words, give the moment its due, by writing a simple three-line haiku prayer.

Prayers of praise—prayers that acknowledge and celebrate the Divine and all its works—arise out of every great faith tradition. These prayers come in many forms, and one form is to simply say *what it is* in creation that fills us with awe.

> Sing to the Lord with thanksgiving;
> make melody to our God on the lyre.
> He covers the heavens with clouds,
>> prepares rain for the earth,
>> makes grass grow on the hills.
> He gives to the animals their food,
>> and to the young ravens when they cry.
>> —PSALM 147:7–9

For a writer, the best praise to receive is not necessarily, "I loved your book." (Though, believe me, that's nice to hear!) The feedback that gives me the greatest joy comes from those who are drawn into my work, have an experience that makes a difference to them, and then tell me about it. They may repeat my own words back to me, but in the context of their lives rather than mine. This expresses the sense that they paid attention and "got it," and these are the conversations that can lift up both of us and send us back to the world renewed in spirit.

> Writing a haiku turns the focus from the all-consuming Me and instead shares one fleeting glimpse of the ever-present Spirit permeating all things.

A haiku is a prayer of praise that celebrates God's work by paying attention and then reflecting back, as simply and clearly as possible, what we experience in God's created world. It is a way of letting God know that we are paying attention, and that, at least for one moment, we "get it."

In my prayer life, so much has to do with *me,* with my immediate concerns and needs. Though I pray for others, it is hard to keep myself out of the picture. *My* hopes for those I love, what *I* think would be best for them, sneaks in whether I am aware of it or not. Writing a haiku offers surprising relief from all that. Writing a haiku turns the focus from the all-consuming Me and instead shares one fleeting glimpse of the ever-present Spirit permeating all things. The relief I feel in turning my focus outward comes not only from escaping the confines of my hungry little self, but also in finding my true self, transformed, in the essence of the world around me.

> When I can enter into the moment at hand and let it speak to me, then I may hear my own heart beat in the rhythms of creation.

> Haiku are an expression of the joy of our reunion with things from which we have been parted by self-consciousness.
>
> —R. H. BLYTH

One of the great Vedic statements in the Hindu Upanishads is *"Tat tvam asi,"* sometimes translated as "Thou art that." In recognizing that the apparent sense of separation between me and everything else is a delusion, these brief and potent words express the oneness between the deepest self and Brahman, or Ultimate Reality. When I can enter into the moment at hand and let it speak to me, then I may hear my own heart beat in

> Wise voices from the ages lift up gratefulness as a way of life for *all* of life, not just the parts that feel good at the time.

the rhythms of creation. Writing a haiku acknowledges and honors the interrelatedness of all things by offering back to the Creator an echo of the heartbeat we all share.

> the spirit, the truth
> of silent prayer—
> just the moon on the road
> —KIKUSHA-NI (1752–1826)

Rise Up and Be Thankful

After seeing the third deer that December afternoon, I wrote my haiku out of a sense of gratitude. It was easy to be grateful at that moment when fear died and courage bloomed. It was much harder to be grateful for the moments that came before. And yet, wise voices from the ages lift up gratefulness as a way of life for *all* of life, not just the parts that feel good at the time.

> O Lord my God, I will give thanks to you forever.
> —PSALM 30:12

> Let us rise up and be thankful, for if we didn't learn a lot today, at least we learned a little, and if we didn't learn a little, at least we didn't get sick, and if we got sick, at least we didn't die; so, let us all be thankful.
> —BUDDHA

> A thankful heart is not only the greatest virtue, but the parent of all other virtues.
> —CICERO

> Certainly the depth and breadth of life's Creation miracle deserves nothing less than our awareness and respect.... And always, our gratitude.
> —JAMES W. HACKETT

Courage it is that endows us with the power to accept gratefully all that happens; Bashō says: "There is nothing you see that is not a flower; there is nothing you can think of which is not the moon."

—R. H. Blyth

I have met a handful of people over the years who seem to live in grace-filled gratitude—individuals who, as far as I can tell, manage to stay in tune with the psalmist singing, "O Lord my God, I will give thanks to you forever," through all the bumps on the road. I am glad that our paths have crossed. They show me what is possible in the life of the Spirit, and I need to be shown. Although I know from personal experience that Love is alive in the heart of every circumstance, ready and waiting to save me yet again, still it remains a struggle for me—at this stage in my spiritual life, anyway—to give thanks in the midst of frustration, pain, heartbreak, or fury.

If I can salute this one dandelion and say something true about it, then I share in the dignity of its being.

In the practice of reading and writing haiku, I find a shortcut into gratitude that feels natural. At its best, haiku shows the way to reverence and thanks by acknowledging things *as they are,* and by letting them be *what they are*—rain as well as sun, crabgrass as well as plum blossoms. If I can salute this one dandelion and say something true about it, then I share in the dignity of its being. A certain peace comes back to me. Within that peace, thanks comes naturally.

weeding—
on my knees
as the earth turns

—Deb Baker

The Pearl of Great Price

Maybe because we long for meaning in life, we human beings are strongly tempted to select, rearrange, and shape what we see to make it fit our own notions of how things ought to be. Writing haiku is a way to face down that temptation. For me, writing a haiku often means waking up again and again from a dream of my own devising, a dream in which I have twisted reality to boost the meaning I want it to have, whether I am aware that that is what I am doing or not.

I do not mean to suggest that we cannot use our imaginations in writing haiku, or that it is wrong to change any detail from the outer world. Haiku is an imaginative art, and from the earliest history of the form, haiku writers have used internal images in their poems, as well as images from direct external experience. Sometimes both are necessary to open the true feeling of the moment to the reader so a poem can be more than just a note to ourselves. As the poet Karma Tenzing Wangchuk, a longtime practitioner of Buddhism, puts it, *makoto:* the sincerity, or poetic truth, for which a haiku poet strives "What isn't the imagination? Everything we see and experience is filtered through and affected by our imaginations. The poet strives for *makoto,* which can be translated as sincerity, or poetic truth."

Unfortunately, I am prone to falling into a pit of insincerity, often motivated by a desire to write the "killer haiku." These motives may feed my ego, but they do not do much for my spirit—or, as it turns out, for my haiku either. If I want my haiku to have *makoto,* I must start by discerning and honoring the underlying feelings of the moment, and to do that, I must pay close attention to what evoked those feelings.

Once again it comes back to faith. Faith that the moment itself is big enough to hold its own meaning. Faith that the pearl of great price is, in fact, just there, in plain sight. It only needs the open eyes of a child to be seen.

So I keep trying gently to bring my mind back to what is really there to be seen, maybe to be seen and noted with a kind of reverence. Because if I don't learn to do this, I think I'll keep getting things wrong.... Let's think of reverence as awe, as presence in and openness to the world.

—ANNE LAMOTT

One cloudy day in winter, I walked along the beach at Point Hudson in downtown Port Townsend. The water of Admiralty Inlet and the sky above it held every shade of gray. The pebble-strewn beach smelled of salt and life. I looked out across the inlet, where one long, low wave after another approached, curled, broke, and dissolved against the shoreline.

It comes back to faith. Faith that the moment itself is big enough to hold its own meaning.

A little girl in a purple jacket ran along the beach in front of me and up to a woman who was standing alone. The woman reached out and drew the child to her. She touched the girl's head, moving her fingers through the girl's red hair as if feeling for a barrette or ribbon that had come undone. I thought she was probably the girl's mother. As I walked by, neither the woman nor the child looked at me. They were involved in each other, and that was enough.

I walked on, watching the breakers curl, and curl. Something moved inside me, a mixture of sorrow and joy that can only be called Mystery. Somehow, the feeling seemed to rise out of a connection between the breakers and the little girl with her mother. I decided to try to capture the moment in a haiku.

Just as a start, I came up with "the curl of the breakers" for the first line. The rest, I thought, would be about the little girl. But what was the connection between the girl and the breakers? My mind puzzled over that question and came up blank. She was a redheaded girl in a purple jacket on a beach. So what? Where was the detail that would turn this moment into a killer haiku?

Immediately, my busy imagination started to offer up things for the little girl to do, things that would show a compelling link between her and the breakers that would be the heart of this haiku.

How about if she were digging in the sand, and a wave comes in and fills the hole? I tried to compose haiku-like lines about that combination of events, involving plastic shovels, sand and sea colliding, red hair and tears against her cheek, but they all took too many words and did not evoke the feeling of the moment at all. I was not writing an ode to the futility of human endeavor.

I was also struck by the pleasing contrast between the girl's purple jacket and her red hair, but could not think of anything to say about it. Hmmm ... how about changing the jacket into a purple hat? (One less syllable!) Lines tumbled forth in which the girl tips her purple cap to the sea, her red hair tousled in the sea air. They still had too many syllables, and none of it evoked sorrow, awe, or Mystery.

My busy, figuring mind figured on, until I finally awoke from the dream, realized what I was doing, and came back to the moment itself, a moment that had come and then passed like the breakers dissolving into the sand-and-pebble beach. What had actually happened? The girl had run to a woman, whom I took to be her mother. I had seen the woman draw the child near and touch her head. Though I liked the girl's purple jacket, I realized that it was not part of the essence of the moment and did not really matter. But somehow, her red hair was part of it and did matter to me. Finally, I wrote this haiku, which, if not a killer, at least is sincere:

> a breaker curls ...
> the woman touches the hair
> of her redheaded child
> —M.D.M.

Did the shape of the child's red curls, echoing the shape of the breakers, spark the link between the child and the ripples of water in my unconscious mind?

Did the depth of my feeling come from a sensed relationship between the mother on the beach and the ocean, the Mother of all life on earth?

Could the power of the moment have to do with my feelings about my own mother, especially now? In the weeks following my mother's stroke, I had more than once combed her hair for her. She was not likely to ever comb mine for me again. Nor would my mother's wheelchair, regardless of the good intentions of anyone trying to push it, be able to negotiate that soft and rocky beach.

Could the power of the moment have to do with my own unborn daughters? I have never been pregnant, a matter of both chance and choice. Now that pregnancy is no longer an option, images of mothers and daughters together reflect back differently than they did when I was young.

> I did not know the answer.... It was good enough to be in the presence of Mystery, and to find myself there.

What was so important about the color of the girl's hair? In my church, red is the liturgical color associated with the third person in the Trinity, the Spirit of God moving and acting on earth. Was her red hair a symbol for me of the One Spirit that connects generations, each to the next?

All those questions grew out of my willingness to spend time with the moment itself. I did not know the answer to any of them, and at the same time, I did not feel that they needed to be answered. It was good enough to be in the presence of Mystery, and to find myself there.

There was one thing I did know: the particular details and events that spoke to me that day were, in some way, mine to see. At any given moment, many things happen. Another person walking the beach that day might have noticed gulls floating on the water, or a flag waving on the bluff, or an odd-shaped rock underfoot. That person's haiku would be very different from mine because that person's moment would be different from mine. The difference lies not in what was happening on the beach, but in who I am and what is happening inside me.

> Who are you trying to please? Someone else? Yourself? Or are you simply trying to record the moment? Everything is coming through our senses at every moment, but we pick out the things we want to see and the things we want to avoid. Writing haiku is a means of chipping away at those habitual behaviors that prevent us from seeing the essence of who we are.
>
> —Christopher Herold

For me that day, writing a haiku was a simple prayer, a prayer that in essence said, "Dear God, here is your work offered back to you. I saw what you have made, and my heart moved inside me. O Lord my God, I will give thanks to you forever. Amen."

Practice: Just the Facts

To see and accept the world just the way it is can be deeply healing—healing both to you and to the world. But before you can find your way to that healing, you will need to put away preconceived notions, let down your guard, and open up to what is really out there. That takes practice, and that is what this practice is all about. In this exercise, you will develop a list of facts—a list of things you perceive to be true. Then you will use your list of true things to write some haiku. In giving your respectful attention to one part of Creation, you will find all that's needed for your haiku to be a simple prayer of praise.

You will need paper and pencil, and at least twenty minutes of quiet time. Give yourself the time you need. *(If you are doing this practice in a group, you will want additional time to share your results with each other.)*

- First, look over the whole practice; then go through the steps one by one.
- If it is practical, go outside and find a place to sit comfortably. If that's not practical, get comfortable where you are.
- Relax, breathe, and look around.
- Jot down the first thing that catches your eye. Identify it specifically. For example, rather than putting down "a tree," say which tree: "the holly tree on the corner."
- Spend a few minutes looking at what you noticed. Open up and take it in. Then write down one objective fact about it that you would not have noticed in a casual glance. You do not need a fancy fact, just a true one. For example, "Holly berries are red in the sun, but they appear black in the shade."
- Keep looking and keep writing until you have *at least* five facts that you would not have noticed about this object in a casual glance.
- If you are outside, write down one quick observation about the current weather. If you are inside, write down one quick observation about the environment of the room. For example, "afternoon sun," or "winter wind," or "fluorescent lights."
- From this material, write a haiku. For your first line, use the one quick observation about the weather or the room. Then choose from among your list of facts to write the next two lines.

Tip: Do not try to cram too much into your haiku. You do not need a new image for each line. In fact, three images in a row can end up reading like a static list. Instead, let your first line set the scene, and then choose one image for the rest of the poem. Write the image in one straight line at first, not worrying about how it will fall into two lines. Look for its essence. Keep the language clear and natural sounding, using no extra words.

- When you feel your image is true and complete, read it out loud. Is there a natural pause between two words? That might be a good place to break it into two lines. Or you might find another place to divide the lines that feels right to you. Now you have the second and third lines of your poem. Try to keep the total length of your haiku to seventeen or fewer syllables.
- Finished? Take a moment to enjoy what you've written. Congratulations on your haiku! *(If you are doing this exercise in a group, give all the group members a chance to share their haiku, if they choose. For tips on reading haiku aloud in a group, see the sidebar on page 23.)*

When you took the time to see more than comes across at first glance, were you surprised by anything you saw? Delighted? Did you see anything that felt like a reflection from your own life? You might see something that reminds you of a current concern, or of a pattern of experiences or choices over many years. When you use that image in a haiku, the practice of writing the haiku may affect how you feel about the issue in your life. Does this feel like prayer to you?

In the coming week, you may want to delve into the images from this practice to write more haiku. Or you can repeat the practice anytime and anywhere you have time to open up to the world and see what is out there.

CHAPTER THREE

A Companionable Form

ancient pond—
frog jumps in
sound of water
    —Matsuo Bashō

As a child at church, my favorite prayers were the responsive kind, those in which the congregation got to join in between the leader's petitions with repeated choruses of "Lord, have mercy," or "Lord, hear our prayer." At the time, I did not know that this was one of the most ancient forms of public prayer. Or, that when we prayed for the welfare of the world and our community, and for healing for all who were sick or suffering, that we were following long-established traditional themes. I only knew that I wanted to pray for those things, and that I could join in the responses with my whole heart.

So, after I grew up and left church—then grew up some more and returned to church—I was happy to find responsive prayers in the Episcopal liturgy, and even happier to find clergy who encourage laypeople like me to write new ones. I read about the history of responsive prayer, which stretches back all the way to the earliest days of community worship, and attended training sessions in which we wrote prayers together as a class. I learned that many diverse prayers used in worship share an underlying form. That form turned out to be a sturdy structure that could support great freedom of expression and imagination in new prayers. I discovered that the more I knew about the form—how it came into being, how its parts fit together, and how its structure and meaning evolved over time—the better I could work within it to create a meaningful experience for others. At the same time, as I got to know the bones holding up the words we all said together in community prayer, those words gained strength, penetrating deeper into my heart and enriching my own spiritual life.

tanka: a two-part Japanese poem containing three lines of five, seven, and five "sound symbols," and two lines of seven

Something similar can happen with haiku. To enjoy reading haiku, and even to start writing haiku, you do not need to know much about the history and structure of the underlying form. But when you find yourself drawn to writing haiku as part of a spiritual practice, then a better understanding of the roots, evolution, traditions, and elements of the form will reveal the surprising depth of these little verses, helping you tap into that depth in your own haiku. Knowing something about what happened when haiku made the leap from Japanese to English and other languages will deepen your reading of classical haiku, so that the old masters can better touch your heart today. Getting to know the bones of the form offers you the freedom to draw from your own spiritual tradition and practice when writing your haiku, at the same time giving you the tools you need to create verses that can move you and others, both today and in years to come.

A History in Love Notes and Other Collaborative Games

Haiku is a friendly little verse form. It mixes well with other forms of art and other kinds of writing, and it provides fun and accessible ways for people to create and share with each other. Given its family history, haiku's friendly nature is hardly surprising. With an ancestry that includes imperial love notes and provincial party games, the lineage of haiku can be traced through centuries of Japanese verse, evolving in ripples of wit, religion, love, spiritual longing, rivalry, and collaboration.

TANKA BEGINNINGS

Before haiku, there was tanka, a form of short verse widely practiced at the Japanese imperial court during the Heian period (ninth to twelfth centuries CE). In Japan's upper classes, poetry writing was not confined to a few folks with literary aspirations. Most everyone at court wrote these brief lyrical poems on all aspects of the human condition, including politics, religion, love, and the ups and downs of daily life. Lovers wrote tanka to express their longing and the pain of separation, usually incorporating into the poem an image from nature to reflect the lover's condition. An exchange of love notes about a hoped-for meeting might be written entirely as one tanka response to another. Ladies kept diaries that included tanka, and competitions were held for the best original tanka. Thousands of the poems were published in popular collections that are still read today.

kireji: Japanese "cutting words" that function something like strong punctuation marks in English

To appreciate the structure of a tanka requires a little background about the Japanese language. Classical Japanese has always been written vertically, without punctuation marks such as periods and commas. Instead, sentence structure is either implied by context or set off by the use of *kireji,* or special "cutting words," which function something like strong punctuation marks in English, such as dashes, colons, and ellipses. Though a tanka appears as a vertical line in Japanese, its internal structure is similar to a five-line poem, and that is how it is usually translated into English.

The first three lines of a tanka contain five, seven, and five "sound symbols," and the final two lines each contain seven. Sound symbols *(on)* are elemental units that comprise Japanese words, with each sound symbol similar in length to the English syllables "be" or "in." Shorter than the average English syllable, these sound symbols also typically hold less information. For those reasons, trying to match the number of Japanese sounds to English syllables does not work very well. A tanka's total of thirty-one sounds might be roughly equivalent to twenty or so syllables in English—still a short poem!

on: the "sound symbols" that comprise Japanese words

The princess who wrote this next seventh-century tanka scribbled a note with the poem that she was "thinking of the Emperor Tenji." The original Japanese, transliterated to the Latin alphabet, appears beside William J. Higginson's English translation.

kimi matsu to	waiting for you
waga koioreba	in longing ...
waga yada no	making the blinds
sudare ugokashi	of my house move
aki no kaze fuku	autumn wind blows
	—PRINCESS NUKUDA

More than a thousand years have passed since Princess Nukuda waited in longing for her lover, and yet her feelings do not feel strange or alien in the modern world—quite the contrary. By connecting her feelings to the autumn wind, whose chilling breezes I have felt every year of my life, her poem leaps across time and space and shares her feelings directly with me. And I suspect that the princess in the Japanese imperial court at Kyoto would have no trouble entering into the feelings expressed in this next tanka, first published near the close of the twentieth century.

> Secret love—
> this town too small
> to let it loose,
> I make confession
> only to the crows.
> —KARMA TENZING WANGCHUK

RENGA: A NEW LINK

Besides playing competitive poetry games, early Japanese poets enjoyed collaborating in verse, a pastime that grew out of the tanka's two-part form. One poet composed the first three lines, and a second poet answered or completed the poem with the last two lines. This two-part poem is known as a *tan renga*. Over time, the pastime evolved into group efforts that produced long poems of alternating 5-7-5 and 7-7 verses called *renga*. Each verse was linked to the one that came before, according to the fancy of the poet who wrote the new verse. *Renga* were often composed at social occasions where people came together to have fun and write poetry as a diversion from the stresses of the day.

tan renga: a two-part Japanese poem created by two different poets, one composing the first three lines in a 5-7-5 pattern and the other, the last two in 7-7

In the early years, *renga* writing was a practice for only the wealthy, literate classes. As the literate middle class expanded, the style of *renga* expanded with it, from the refined tones of the court to playful, witty, and even bawdy variations called *haikai no renga*. Rules developed for writing *renga* and in time grew very complex, until finally the host of a *renga* party would be likely to hire a professional poet or teacher to oversee the creative process.

It was in this lively milieu of writing poetry as a social game that the peculiar character of haiku began to take shape, growing out of the requirements for the *renga's* three-line starting verse, called the *hokku*. Written in the 5-7-5 pattern, the *hokku* served as a launching point, setting a tone that would develop and evolve through the course of the long poem. It always included a reference to the current season, often with a graceful nod to the host of the event, and conveyed an open feeling, fit for the start of a long and varied poetic journey. Because it was the *renga's* most important verse, poets often composed *hokku* ahead of time to bring with them to poetry events, hoping for the honor of having their verse chosen to start the *renga*.

> *renga:* long poems of alternating 5-7-5 and 7-7 verses, often composed at social occasions by a group of people

---

Is it a haiku or a *senryū*?

A *senryū* is similar in structure to haiku but focused more closely on human nature. Traditionally, a *senryū* does not contain the haiku's grammatical shift, and it may not contain a seasonal reference either. Often, a *senryū* will poke a little fun at the human condition.

> Stumbling in the dark,
> then fumbling for the light switch,
> which turns on the fan.
> —Gregory Frederick

Although the everyday situation and smile-inducing images in Gregory Frederick's three-line poem are consistent in tone with many traditional haiku, students of the form will likely call it a *senryū*, not a haiku, because of its subject matter. If you are just starting to write haiku, the difference between the forms may not matter to you at this point. But if you find yourself writing a lot of haiku and wanting to submit your work for publication in a haiku journal, it will help you to get a feel for the distinctions. Some magazines publish both haiku and *senryū*; others specialize in one or the other. A number of publications issue guidelines that will tell you more about the nuances of what makes a haiku a haiku, and a *senryū* a *senryū*.

HAIKU'S EMERGENCE

The recognition of *hokku* as an independent verse form took place gradually, over the course of many years. By the fifteenth century, published *renga* sometimes included additional *hokku* that were listed separately from the main poem. The seventeenth-century poet Bashō, a respected teacher and popular leader of *renga* events, kept travel journals that included *hokku* written for *renga* parties he attended on his journeys. Bashō later revised his travel journals for publication, editing, deleting, and adding *hokku* throughout the work.

hokku: a *renga's* starting verse, which included a reference to the current season

Today, Bashō's verses appear in virtually every compilation of classic haiku, and he is widely acknowledged as one of the great masters, if not the greatest master, of the form. Still, after his death, another two hundred years would pass before haiku was formally recognized as an independent form of poetry. It was the nineteenth-century poet Masaoka Shiki who proposed treating this *hokku* offshoot of the *renga* as its own separate self. Shiki named the new form "haiku."

Along with its 5-7-5 structure, the haiku form preserved the *hokku's* seasonal reference, as well as a feeling of openness that invited the reader into the poem. A haiku might be grammatically incomplete, giving the sense of a fleeting moment in time. Haiku also preserved the convention in *hokku* of putting a single grammatical shift (break) or *kireji* (cutting word) at the end of the first or the second line. The break serves to separate and relate two elements in the haiku, while dividing the poem into two slightly unequal parts. In English, the break is often indicated by a dash, a colon, or an ellipsis, or it may be present with no punctuation to mark it.

In this winter haiku, an image of deep cold, coupled with the quiet of early morning, captures a moment that feels both unique and timeless—simply itself. The seasonal reference is "snowflakes," and the break occurs after the second line.

> snowflakes
> frozen to tree-bark
> morning silence
> —DORIS HORTON THURSTON

Over centuries of Japanese verse, certain natural elements or events became associated with a particular season because they evoke the *feeling* of the season, even though they might be present at any time of the year. For example, the pheasant, a year-round resident of Japan, became poetically associated with spring because the pheasant's colors are brighter and its song is most often heard during spring's mating season.

> sunrise …
> the male pheasant
> owns the road
> —ALICE FRAMPTON

For traditionalists, this would be considered a spring haiku, although as the poet Alice Frampton remarks, "Any time a male pheasant would be on the road we would stop to look and give him room to strut." The break occurs at the end of the first line.

Haiku was first translated into English near the end of the nineteenth century. Throughout the twentieth century these little poems traveled and made friends all over the world, and haiku is now, arguably, the most popular type of verse being written today. Although it continues to evolve as a form, haiku's long lineage remains in its DNA, and its near relations persist in new life. Around the world, friends gather to write linked verse poems (now commonly called *renku*), and new tanka continue to distill the joys and sorrows of the human condition in five brief lines.

Translating from Culture to Culture

When the *Princeton Tiger* magazine published this limerick in 1924, it received an enthusiastic response from readers all along the Eastern seaboard. Many wrote and sent in sequels that were printed in periodicals from the *Pawtucket Times* to the *Chicago Tribune*.

> There once was a man from Nantucket
> Who kept all his cash in a bucket.
> But his daughter, named Nan,
> Ran away with a man
> And as for the bucket, Nantucket.

At first glance, the haiku and the limerick might not appear to have much in common, other than both being brief forms of poetry. Yet, if you take a closer look, the likenesses reveal themselves, illuminating some of the challenges faced in translating verse not only from language to language but also from culture to culture.

Each of the two forms produces short verses with a particular internal structure; each has deep roots in its own culture's soil; each achieved popularity across class boundaries; and each gives all sorts of people pleasure in the creative act of writing verse. With so much in common, you might guess that haiku and limerick could travel with ease back and forth between their lands and cultures. But before packing its bags, take another look at the limerick about the man from Nantucket. Given what you know of the Japanese language, how would you go about translating that poem into Japanese?

> The indefinable feeling that lives and breathes in the finest classic haiku is caught in the essence of a passing moment, a moment utterly itself and like nothing else.

What do you do about the limerick's rollicking beat? What about the rhyme scheme? The limerick sounds natural in English because it fits with the English language. How would you make it sound as natural in Japanese? Each sound symbol in Japanese has the same length, and Japanese words are accented by pitch, not by stressed and unstressed accents, as in English. Poetry in Japanese is customarily built around combinations of sound patterns, such as 5-7-5 and 7-7, not rhythmic patterns and rhymes.

Then what do you do about *Nantucket,* a New England place name derived from a Native American term? The word has a resonance in American ears with echoes that extend far back in our national history, a resonance that would be lost in translation. Transported into a different culture, *Nantucket* is no more than an odd combination of meaningless sounds.

Most difficult of all—what about the joke? Would the translated poem still be funny? And if not funny, could it still be called a limerick?

These are exactly the kinds of issues that translators face when translating Japanese haiku into English.

The 5-7-5 sound pattern in Japanese has no direct and natural equivalent in English. It sounds right in Japanese because it rises out of characteristics that are built into the language. Recognizing this, many early translators abandoned any attempt to mimic the 5-7-5 pattern, and some made free translations that used meter and rhyme to create poems they hoped would "sound natural" to native English speakers. These were valiant efforts; however, they simply did not read or feel much like haiku.

Other early translators decided to keep the 5-7-5 pattern and equate one Japanese sound symbol with one English syllable, rendering haiku into strict three-line verses of five, seven, and five syllables. This approach created poems with a structure easy to grasp in English while at the same time being a distinctly new form, not a hybrid of existing English forms. Skilled poet-translators wrote beautiful and evocative translations that enjoyed wide popularity. The form caught on, and new haiku were written in English using the 5-7-5 syllable structure. You may have been introduced to haiku in this form, and you will frequently see the haiku form defined in this way.

> In sharing haiku with others, we discover that we are not alone in our feelings, but that sorrow, joy, and all that comes between are part of the universal human spirit.

However, because Japanese sound symbols are both shorter in length than most English syllables and typically hold less information, haiku translated or written in lines of 5-7-5 English syllables are longer than Japanese haiku—sometimes much longer. Here is the original Japanese of Bashō's famous frog pond haiku, side-by-side with a rendering of the poem in three lines of seventeen syllables:

Furu ike ya	The quiet old pond ...
kawazu tobikomu	from the shore, a frog jumps in
mizu no oto	to a fresh *kersplash!*

The difference in the overall length of the two poems would be no big deal, if it weren't that brevity matters so much in haiku.

The landscape of haiku lies close at hand.

Adding words for no better reason than to get the right syllable count runs contrary to the spirit and essence of the form. A skillful poet-translator might make a fine poem in seventeen syllables, but the verse will inevitably gain a little weight in transition. Some of the slender quality of the underlying work is lost.

Translators face yet another challenge in dealing with the places and season words that appear throughout Japanese haiku. Places of national historic and religious importance often appear by name in Japanese haiku. Like *Nantucket,* these place names evoke complex cultural memories that are lost in translation. References to the current season in Japanese haiku also carry a rich mix of poetic and spiritual meaning, fed by allusions that are spread across a millennium of poetry and religious practice. To convey only a fraction of all these resonances, some translators include footnotes many times the length of the poem itself.

And most difficult of all—what about the indefinable feeling that lives and breathes in the finest classic haiku? This feeling is caught in the essence of a passing moment, a moment utterly itself and like nothing else, in the same instant that all it holds is changing and passing away.

> The basic tenet of Buddhism, that of *mujō,* or impermanence, is naturally reflected in most haiku.... Haiku, which usually refers to nature, depicts it not as "fallen," as in the West, but transient; there is an acceptance and appreciation of its evanescence. In Japanese aesthetics this is called *aware,* or sad beauty.
>
> —PATRICIA DONEGAN

The essence and poignancy of this feeling is as hard to describe as what makes a joke funny. And yet, if the translated poem doesn't have it, then part of what makes the poem a haiku is lost.

All these and more features of Japanese haiku have required time and study to be revealed in translation. In the decades since haiku first appeared in English, techniques for translating them have evolved, along with understanding of the underlying form.

The graceful contemporary translation of Bashō's famous frog pond haiku that appears at the start of this chapter is true to the original in meaning and substance, and it takes about as long to say out loud.

> ancient pond—
> frog jumps in
> sound of water
> —MATSUO BASHŌ

In spite of the many challenges, haiku has shown itself to be strong enough to move from language to language and culture to culture, taking root and thriving wherever it goes. In reading and writing haiku, people who live in deserts and rain forests, coastlands and inlands, all can find a common path to feeling and expressing their inner connections to the natural world. In sharing haiku with others, we discover that we are not alone in our feelings, but that sorrow, joy, and all that comes between are part of the universal human spirit.

So What Makes It a Haiku?

As the preceding pages show, a simple count of lines and syllables cannot describe haiku as a form. A better way might be to list a few of haiku's principle traits, along with a variety of examples. Such a list is always subjective, both in what it includes and in what it leaves out. I chose these traits because, to my eyes, they draw a picture of the form as it is written in English today. And I chose these examples because I like them.

Here are some of the traits that make a haiku a haiku:

- *A haiku is brief.* In English, haiku are usually written in three lines of seventeen or fewer syllables. Some translators have suggested that about twelve syllables in English are roughly equivalent to seventeen Japanese sound symbols. Ideally, a haiku offers up the essence of a passing moment, without an excess of words to come between the reader and the moment.

> clear water is cool
> fireflies vanish—
> there's nothing more
> —CHIYO-NI (1703–1755)

- *A haiku uses images to talk about everyday things.* Grounded in time and space, haiku evoke feeling through the language of senses and images, with a focus on the stuff of ordinary life. The landscape of haiku lies close at hand. The language of haiku is plain and direct. As Christopher Herold puts it, "Haiku are most effective when in their element: being awed by seemingly insignificant things, say, a pale ray of sunlight illuminating a clump of dust in a corner." Often, an image from nature conveys a link between the natural world and human nature. Seasonal images, such as plum blossoms for spring or icicles for winter, are commonly used to help anchor the poem in time. Whether a haiku is set in a wilderness, backyard, city street, or kitchen, sharp and clear images are its lifeblood.

> A bitter morning:
> sparrows sitting together
> without any necks
> —JAMES W. HACKETT

- *A haiku has an open feeling.* Like a fleeting moment that is gone before we quite grasp it, a haiku is not expected to answer every question that it asks. Most haiku contain a grammatical break or shift that keeps the internal structure from wrapping itself up in a neat little package. The break also provides readers an opening to enter into the poem and intuit their own connections between the images.

> heart-shaped stone
> snow melting over
> into cold earth
> —M.D.M.

- *Haiku shows things as they are.* The images in a haiku speak for themselves, without an overlay of explanations or interpretations. Bashō said, "Learn of the pine from the pine; learn of the bamboo from the bamboo." By noticing and expressing the simple truth of things, the haiku poet respects and honors the world we live in together. By showing things as they are, the poet helps us see ourselves as well.

> dark, dark night
> a leaf strikes the pavement
> stem first
> —CHRISTOPHER HEROLD

Brief images of everyday things are shown just as they are in a fleeting moment. Sometimes I wonder how anything so simple can make a difference in my spiritual life. And yet, with no more than these basic elements, a haiku has the power to take me out of my fussy, worrywart brain and bring me back to earth, back to this moment, and back to life.

The story is told that when Bashō was studying Zen Buddhism, his teacher criticized him for spending so much time writing poetry, feeling that it distracted Bashō from his studies. In his defense, Bashō told the monk that haiku was nothing more than "what happens at this place and at this moment." Struck by his reply, Bashō's teacher recognized that there was no conflict with the practice of Zen, which focuses on direct experience as the path to enlightenment rather than creeds, scriptures, and dogma. After their exchange, the monk let the subject alone, and Bashō continued writing his haiku.

> The crux of writing haiku is recognizing what is right in front of you, writing it down, then stepping back to see all that was hidden.

Other faith traditions also lift up attention to the present moment for those who seek a whole spiritual life. In the book of Matthew, Jesus is quoted as saying, "Do not worry about tomorrow, for tomorrow will bring worries of its own. Today's trouble is enough for today" (Matt. 6:34). And the gnostic Gospel of Thomas quotes Jesus as saying, "Recognize what is right in front of you, and that which is hidden from you will be revealed to you. Nothing hidden will fail to be displayed."

The crux of writing haiku is recognizing what is right in front of you, writing it down, then stepping back to see all that was hidden before you took the time to really look.

Practice: In Defense of Good Form

From the earliest days, haiku poets grappled with tension between following the "rules" of the form and breaking free from them. In a letter to a student, Bashō, the first great haiku master, advised that as long as a verse sounded right, the poet should not worry too much about a few extra syllables. However, Bashō wrote, "If even one syllable stagnates in your mouth, give it a careful scrutiny." The nineteenth-century poet Masaoka Shiki explicitly told beginners to disregard the old rules. And yet, both he and Bashō composed hundreds of haiku that closely follow the form's conventions, many of which appear in anthologies of the best haiku ever written.

The conventions of the haiku form—the structure and other traits that make a haiku a haiku—are like a craftsperson's tools. The more familiar they are to you, the better they can help you find and express the truth of your own unique encounters in the life of the Spirit. Just remember that the form exists as your tool, and not as your trap.

> I'm breaking the rules—
> no nature images, no
> quick revelation
> —*Barbara Gibson*

I am particularly fond of this poem by Barbara Gibson, not only for its spirited attitude toward "the rules," but also because its naturally flowing words fit exactly in three lines of five, seven, and five syllables, with a break at the end of the first line.

When I first encountered haiku, the discipline of honing and clarifying my words down to seventeen syllables helped me hone and clarify my thoughts and feelings, too. The following practice, In Defense of Good Form, is all about using the form as a tool to help you figure out what you want to say and then say it as clearly as you can. To do that, you will take a close look at an everyday tool that you already know well.

In addition to paper and pencil, you will need a favorite tool you use in an activity that you enjoy. Choose a fairly simple object that helps you make or shape physical things, such as a tool from the kitchen, workbench, studio, or sewing basket. *(If you plan to do this practice in a group, ask group members to bring a favorite tool with them to the meeting.)* You will need at least twenty minutes of quiet time. Give yourself the time you need. *(If you are doing this practice in a group, you will want additional time to share your results with each other.)*

- First, look over the whole practice; then go through the steps one by one.
- Get comfortable where you are. Relax, breathe, and look around.
- Now examine your favorite tool as if you were seeing it for the first time. Pick it up and turn it over. Look at it from all sides.
- Write down a factual description of the object. Record everything that you observe about it, including its color and shape, what it is made of, and where it shows signs of use. Take at least ten minutes to describe it as thoroughly as you can. Try sketching it; you might see this familiar object in a new way. *(If you are doing this practice in a group, consider exchanging objects before you start, so that you are describing the tool someone else brought. You might be surprised at what you find—and at what another person sees in an object that you know very well.)*
- Using your observations for ideas and material, write a haiku that includes the tool in some way. Follow these conventions in writing your haiku:
  - Include a reference to the current month or season. The seasonal reference could be as simple as "Spring morning" or "New Year's Eve." A reference from nature is okay as long as it indicates the current season, such as "harvest moon" for autumn or "snow flurries" for winter. For ideas, look outside and see what's going on right now.
  - Put a break or grammatical shift at the end of *either* the first or second line, but *not both*. One break, not two.

- Keep your poem at seventeen or fewer syllables, and make the second line a bit longer than the first and third.
- For extra credit, try writing an eleven-syllable haiku, with lines of three, five, and three syllables each. Or, if you are more comfortable counting accents or beats, write a haiku with two accented syllables in the first line, three accents in the middle line, and two in the third line.

• Finished? Take a moment to enjoy what you've written. Congratulations on your haiku! *(If you are doing this exercise in a group, give all the group members a chance to share their haiku if they choose.)*

Did you learn anything about your favorite tool that you may not have noticed before putting it in a haiku? What did you learn about yourself, how you use tools, and what you might create with them?

When first introduced to writing haiku, my friend Brad told me that he expected to find the form limiting. Instead, as he worked on his haiku it kept changing "almost as if it had a mind of its own," opening the way to unexpected ideas and deeper associations. As you worked within the form, did your haiku change in ways that you did not expect? What insights came to you out of those changes?

In the coming week, follow the conventions of the form when you write new haiku. Experiment with putting a break at the end of the first line or the second line. Play with the various conventions until they become comfortable tools in your hands.

Chapter Four

A Sense of Time and Place

The time it takes—
for snowflakes to whiten
the distant pines.
                    —Lorraine Ellis Harr (1912–2006)

A light snow was falling. It was thirty years and six months ago as I write these words. David and I stood on the sidewalk of Highland Avenue between Carey and North Streets in Sidney, Ohio. Across the street, tired white two-storey houses lined the east side of Highland. On our side of the block, the old brick factory of the Sidney Machine Tool Company stretched from corner to corner. David was home from college for Christmas break. I had made the trip from Seattle to be with my family for the holidays. Though my friendship with this hometown boy had deepened in the past year, it was just in the past few days—just in the past few hours, sitting and talking in the family room of my parents' house, just in the past few minutes, as I walked him partway home—that I sensed something big might be happening. We were taking tentative steps into a new relationship.

We had been talking for hours, and I needed time alone. I told David I was turning back home. He put his arms around me and hugged me close to him. We were both wearing puffy winter coats, and the thick layers of fabric pressed together between us. He kissed me. It was not my first kiss, or his first kiss. It was *our* first kiss. His lips were warm. Snowflakes touched my face with tiny sparks of cold and instantly melted.

We drew apart and said our goodbyes. David turned and walked away, heading across town for the house where he grew up. I turned and walked back to the house where my parents lived. In a few days, he would fly back to New Haven to complete his senior year at Yale, and I would fly back to my job in Seattle. I did not know what would happen next or when we would see each other again. I did know that the road had turned.

numen: a spirit that inhabits and gives life to a place, an object, or a natural happening

On that late-December afternoon in 1978, that block on Highland Avenue did not feel sacred to me. I was too full of puzzlement, hope, doubt, and happiness to give a second thought to anything outside myself. It is only in memory, after thirty years of life with David, that I recognize that particular place and moment as numinous.

A numen is a spirit that inhabits and gives life to a place, an object, or a natural happening. The word's Latin root means both "divine power" and "a nod of the head."

kami: in the Shinto faith, spirits that dwell within objects and forces of nature

Although the English word *numen* has its roots in the *numina* of the ancient Roman religion, the idea of a spirit or life-energy inherent in the things around us—in a waterfall, the moon, the autumn wind—appears in ancient religions and philosophy all around the world. In Japan's native Shinto faith, spirits that dwell within objects and forces of nature are called *kami*.

The monotheistic religions carry the idea of indwelling spirit forward through the all-pervading idea of the numinous. A numinous place is one where the presence of God is felt and known. In this place, God nods in our direction, and we become aware of the Spirit's presence and the link between us.

> Behold! In the creation of the heavens and the earth; in the alternations of the night and the day; in the sailing of the ships through the ocean for the profit of human beings; in the rain which God sends down from the skies, and the life which God gives therewith to a land that is dead; in the beasts of all kinds that God scatters through the earth; in the change of the winds, and the clouds employed between sky and earth, surely there are signs for people that are wise.
>
> —QUR'AN 2:164

So ... where and when can encounters with the numinous happen? Where might we have a sense of the sacred in life?

The answer seems to be—any place and anytime. Although I believe that is true, I don't find the answer very satisfying. Because I can't remember *any* place or *any* time. I remember *that* place and *this* time.

What do I remember about that snowy Ohio day years ago? The season—white snow falling through gray light. A particular place in my hometown—the street block, the dark red brick of the old factory, so dark with soot and age it was nearly black. The muffled press of thick fabric against my body. The touch of snowflakes on my cheek. David's lips against mine.

> snow flurries
> beside the machine shop
> lips touch * a spark
>   —M.D.M.

In naming particular elements of the time and place along with what happened there, this haiku contains the heart of the moment for me. Even now, after so many years, its words can bring that moment back to spontaneous life. Even now, a numen makes its home in each and every one of these things, and Love nods her head.

A Sense of Time

In the American Midwest where I grew up, forsythia is a har-binger of spring. When all else is still gray and brown, the for-sythia puts out its brilliant yellow blooms, and spring has arrived. My brother, Brian, who moved out to Seattle a few years after I did, has a forsythia bush in his backyard. Our grand-mother gave it to his family to commemorate the birth of their first son. Although forsythia grows in the Pacific Northwest, it is not as common as it is in the Midwest, so the sight of my brother's forsythia in bloom can be a singular springtime event for me. It brings back sensory memories of springs long past, and in so doing, this one yellow bush evokes the spirit of Spring itself. For my brother, its blooms also bring memories of our late grandmother, connecting one generation to the next.

a numinous place:
where the presence of
God is felt and known

Lilacs come into flower a little later than forsythia, nearer to the transition between spring and summer. We had a big lilac bush in our backyard at my childhood home. Every year when the lilacs bloomed, my mother would cut a generous bouquet for me to take to my teacher at school. I felt so proud, walking to school with this bountiful gift and offering it to my teacher, who put the purple flowers in a big glass vase, their heady aroma filling the classroom. My hometown today on the Olympic Peninsula is full of huge lilac bushes. When they come into bloom, I see them everywhere, and I am again taken back to springs long past, and to transitions in life—transitions between spring and summer, and between one stage of knowing and the next.

Although I am far from my youth in Ohio in both time and place, when the forsythia blooms in my brother's backyard and the lilacs bloom here in Port Townsend, yesterday and today meet to make a whole life.

My associations with forsythia and lilacs feel very personal to me, and yet I know that at some level, I share the *experience* of forsythia and lilacs with everyone who lives where they bloom. Part of the power of that experience comes from the simple fact that seasons come back regularly. When spring returns, events in the natural world wake us up from our winter doldrums and remind us of springs past. Returning sports events, such as the basketball play-offs, and holidays, such as St. Valentine's Day and Easter, add interpersonal, social, and religious memories to the mix. At the same time, new experiences are busily creating new memories that deepen associations with the season in coming years.

> In haiku, a moment of personal insight can be set in the context of a universal aspect of a season, each drawing energy from the other.

<blockquote>
once again
the scent of lilacs
mother's call to supper
—JOHN SOULES
</blockquote>

In haiku, a moment of personal insight can be set in the context of a universal aspect of a season, each drawing energy from the other. A reference to a season brings with it the potential to tap into deeply personal and shared communal associations with one brief image. Over centuries of verse writing in Japan, a body of recognized season words developed, becoming a standard part of the haiku form. Called *kigo,* these words and phrases are collected in seasonal almanacs *(saijiki),* which are widely used by present-day haiku clubs in Japan.

kigo: a body of recognized season words developed in Japan that became a standard part of the haiku form

Many *kigo* reach far back in Japan's religious and cultural history. According to Patricia Donegan, "The *kigo* most likely has shaman/Shinto roots, for tanka poetry, the precursor to haiku, has its origins in spells and chants to evoke the deities. Haiku is a way to call the spirit of the thing named, whether it be the spring rain or full moon."

Standard collections of season words have not developed in English poetics the way they have in Japanese. Still, the words and images that bring to mind a particular time of year have the power to evoke keen personal and universal feelings in any language, calling forth the spirit of the season.

In this haiku, a breezy moment in spring is the context for a sudden awareness of the poet's own mortality.

> spring wind—
> I too
> am dust
> —PATRICIA DONEGAN

Even something as small and simple as dust carries with it deep and multilayered associations. For me, this haiku has powerful associations with the Ash Wednesday service, one of my favorite early-spring liturgies in the Christian calendar. On Ash Wednesday, the priest draws a cross of ashes on my forehead, saying the words, "Remember that you are dust, and to dust you shall return."

For the poet, writing haiku relates to her practice of Zen meditation. She finds a connection between the two in "being able to appreciate ... daily life, to slow down and be present in the moment." Writing "spring wind," Donegan says, "was one of those genuine haiku moments when I felt the dust blowing in the spring wind against my screen window in Tokyo, in the midst of greening buds, and suddenly felt I was getting older and was impermanent as dust, too, a part of life's cycle."

saijiki: collections of *kigo* in seasonal almanacs

With the turning of the seasons, natural objects change, reflecting changes in our lives. This autumn haiku evokes the passing of a season with a sense of great peace.

> This leaf too, with all
> its colors eaten into lace,
> floats on the stream
> —JAMES W. HACKETT

In this poem, the word *too* ties the leaf image to the poet, and through him to me, floating along my own river of life. It reminds me that even when I feel "eaten up" by life, a beautiful pattern may be revealed in the process.

The universal and the personal also come together in our experiences of seasonal foods, bringing a rich assortment of memory and feelings. A haiku could be written in the kitchen while cooking, smelling, or tasting a favorite dish of a holiday meal. Or it could germinate, come to flower, and bear fruit in the course of a long, sunny walk.

> end of summer—
> shirt pockets
> full of plums
> —KARMA TENZING WANGCHUK

Certain events and chores of daily life at home are also tied to the changing seasons. In this spring haiku, a common seasonal task turns into a lively contest with a broom. (Or at least, that's what happens in my mind's eye.) The image lightens the job and puts a smile on my face.

> spring cleaning
> some spiders move quickly
> some don't
>
> —JAY HASKINS

Often, a change in the season uncovers items that may live in storage for most of the year. For example, each year on March 14, my father's birthday, I get the hummingbird feeder out of the tool shed, fill it with sugar water, and hang it out on the deck. We usually see our first hummingbird of the season within a day or two.

Objects linked to major holidays may carry extra meaning and emotional resonance. The following winter haiku records a small moment at the end of a larger seasonal task that repeats each year.

> winter's eve
> we hang the last ornament
> way to the back
>
> —M.D.M.

This poem comes from a moment when I saw the last ornament, a hand-carved wooden rabbit, being hung in shadow, for no other reason than that it was last out of the box. Writing this haiku, I decided to use the generic word *ornament* rather than a more descriptive phrase, so that an ornament from the reader's own childhood or family collection could spring to mind.

Even something as small and simple as dust carries with it deep and multilayered associations.

These haiku show how seasons of nature can bring the universal and the personal together in a moment that evokes vivid feeling. The cyclical changes of our lives have the same power. Moving away from home for the first time, for example, may seem like a singular event when it happens, but for many of us, variations on its feelings of passage will return again and again as we revolve through the stages of life: having a child, taking a new job, returning to school, attending a wedding, watching at a deathbed.

> Haiku show how seasons of nature can bring the universal and the personal together in a moment that evokes vivid feeling.

In this next haiku, many stages of life come together in one poignant moment that could take place in any season.

> circle of lamplight—
> I complete the baby quilt
> begun for me
> —CAROLYN HALL

Where each of us is today on our spiritual path springs from all that has come before—every touch, conversation, and event. Each experience takes place at a specific point in time, a moment alive with the Spirit. By situating a haiku in its own season, we can tap into the depth of generations that are contained in the essence of one moment, at the same time opening a door for feeling from the past to come into the present and touch us again.

A Sense of Place

If a season reference, such as spring wind or a pocket full of plums, fixes a haiku in time, a place reference, such as mountain peaks or desert sand, locates the poem in physical space. And just as deep feelings become entwined in seasonal events as they come and go, the feelings generated by a life-changing event have a tendency to bond with the place where it occured. A visit to the place, or even the sound of its name, evokes an emotional memory of what happened there.

So, for me, one block of Highland Avenue in Sidney, Ohio, brings back a peculiar blend of uncertainty and hope that is new love.

For my country, the place name "Gettysburg" carries a complex mix of national division, sorrow, identity, and unity that lives on in both time and place. The Civil War battle fought there changed the course of the conflict that threatened to tear the country apart; Lincoln's great speech helped define the nation that emerged from that war; and today the Gettysburg National Military Park welcomes thousands of visitors every year. Browsing through the park's website, I came upon a picture of a tall, split-rail fence set in a large field of green summer grass. The fence reminded me of stories of Abraham Lincoln splitting rails in his youth, and the following haiku rose out of the image of a fence that both divides and joins wide fields of grass.

> Gettysburg ...
> a split-rail fence crosses over
> fields of summer grass
>
> —M.D.M.

Writing the phrase "summer grass," I was also thinking of Bashō's "summer grasses" haiku, which he wrote after a visit to the site of a historic event that occurred during a time of internal power struggles in Japan (see page 18). From the very start of Japan's long poetic tradition, places revered for their historic events, scenic beauty, or religious significance were named or described in poems. Over time, a number of such places became recognized for evoking particular poetic feelings and associations. Used by Japanese poets as a kind of shorthand for tapping into shared cultural sensibilities, a body of such place names came to be called *utamakura,* or "poetic pillows." Poets and poetry lovers planned trips to the locations of their favorite poems to experience the places first-hand, making them popular travel destinations in Japan. A poet might write new haiku to commemorate such a visit, deepening the poetic associations of the place over time. Particularly beloved poems were carved into stones and placed at the site where the poem was written. Old and new "haiku stones" can be found all over Japan—in parks and on the grounds of ancient temples and shrines, on the streets of Tokyo and along remote country lanes.

> *utamakura:* a body of place names, or "poetic pillows," used for tapping into shared cultural sensibilities

Like *saijiki* (the collections of *kigo,* or season words), a body of recognized *utamakura* has been a standard part of the haiku form in Japan for generations. While reading about the Japanese tradition of recognizing sacred places in poetry, I began to wonder which spots in my hometown or country might make good "poetic pillows"—places that evoke feelings common to the community or larger culture. Locations that were significant to me, personally, came to mind, but the more I thought about it, the more I realized any list I came up with by myself could not tell me what I wanted to know.

So I sent a little informal, unscientific e-mail survey to about fifty of my friends in and around Port Townsend. In the survey, I asked my friends to name five places in the immediate vicinity of town that were sacred to them, either for personal reasons or for the community at large. I also asked them to name five places outside their local area and within the United States that were sacred to them, either personally or for the nation. Then I sat back and waited for the data to roll in.

And roll in it did. If I did not know it before, here is one piece of news about the human family that came through loud and clear in responses to the survey: we are connected to planet Earth by more than the force of gravity. We are tied to the places of our lives by the forces that shape and ground our hearts and spirits.

We are connected to planet Earth by more than the force of gravity. We are tied to the places of our lives by the forces that shape and ground our hearts and spirits.

My survey asked for no more than brief lists of place names, and that is what many sent back. Quite a few others wanted to write more. Some wrestled with the word *sacred,* and some wanted to tell me why one place or another ended up on their lists. Many responses connected sacredness to places of great natural beauty. Some connected sacred places with times in life when emotions are close to the surface, especially feelings of deep sorrow and comfort.

A few people did not answer my survey, and a few others sent short responses explaining that they did not feel qualified to answer. After thanking me for thinking of her, one woman said that she just didn't have any sacred places, explaining that she was "rather stunted in the spiritual department." Then, a couple of hours after receiving that response, I received a second reply from her. She wrote, "I can give one answer. I think the Vietnam Memorial is a sacred place for our nation. Not because it memorializes a war, but because it brings that war home in a very personal way. I have read that everyone falls into silence as they approach it. For whatever reason, it seems to evoke that universal response."

For someone who doesn't think much of her own spiritual height, she certainly grasped what I was looking for when I sent out the survey.

In short, a wonderfully varied set of places came back from my informal poll, and with the places, the feelings people held about these sacred spots. Because writing a haiku is a way to share both the essence of a moment and the feeling it evokes, patterns in these feelings are just as interesting to the haiku poet as the places themselves. If we can better understand what it is about these sacred places that gives meaning to human life, we are better able to offer back that meaning in our haiku.

From the wealth of material that people sent me, I tried to group the responses into categories to make sense of it all. Finding patterns helped reveal what the word *sacred* means to different people. Three general categories of feelings connected to sacred places became apparent:

- a sense of belonging, or home
- a sense of awe, or wonder
- a sense of wholeness, or healing from division

What makes a place sacred?

"A sacred place, for me, is anywhere I am, when I am paying attention." —Rachel

"I see the whole earth as sacred." —Polly

"I don't find places themselves sacred. How I am, who I am with, if I am overtly seeking God—all of these can bring sacredness to any moment and place in my life." —Elisabeth

"I think places where you can cry are sacred." —Willene

"My first thought about sacred places has to do with nature.... It seems to me that whenever I am in a place with great grandeur, I think about God and creation, and my relationship with the world—which makes that place sacred to me." —Ginny

---

A SENSE OF BELONGING, OR HOME

Often, the places that people named in my survey were very familiar to the person who responded. These included childhood haunts, places where friends meet or family gathers, and places where connections have grown over time and by custom. Favorite walks near a current residence were mentioned, as well as favorite walks from long ago.

Karen, who grew up in Port Townsend, included on her list "the bridge crossing at the end of the stream at Chetzemoka Park. It has been sacred to me since I have any memory and have all these years wandered to it for meditation, pondering, and prayer. It remains the most sacred place in my life." Bill, a retired park ranger, put the Pennsylvania Game Department's Middle Creek Wildlife Management Area on his list, "especially walks to Willow Point along the paved accessible trail, pushing my mother in her wheelchair."

> The places where we have a sense of belonging, a sense of home, come to hold feelings that can stretch from sorrow to joy and all that lies between.

People listed as sacred their own homes, gardens, and vacation cabins. One friend's musings about sacred places boiled down to a single entry: his bed with his wife in it. Over time, the places where we have a sense of belonging, a sense of home, come to hold feelings that can stretch from sorrow to joy and all that lies between. This gentle evening haiku evokes a sense of both *now* and *then* in one poignant, homey moment.

> my bed companions:
> gray cat, hot water bottle,
> dreams of long-lost loves
> —BARBARA GIBSON

A SENSE OF AWE, OR WONDER

Places that evoke awe at the wonder of creation, particularly places of striking natural beauty, are regarded as holy by peoples across history and around the world. Cathedrals and monuments are structures we build to evoke the same kinds of feelings. In my survey results, the Olympic Mountains and specific places in the mountain range appeared on many lists, with one typical comment speaking of being "awestruck by the spirit felt there."

The earth's waters also evoke feelings of awe and wonder. Ginny wrote about kayaking around Port Townsend's beaches: "Awesome feeling the power of the sea, seeing the kelp beds and crab, and Mount Baker in the background. There's something about water ... that gives a place sacredness." Rachel also evoked water's power when she named Niagara Falls: "Not much can upstage the glory of this awesome sight, full of roaring sound and drenching mists." John wrote of standing at the northwest tip of the Olympic Peninsula and looking out across Tatoosh Island "to the vast, far spaces of the North Pacific and an intimation of the forevers of this world."

Part of the sense of awe attached to these places comes from the physical sense of being there, and in some cases, simply getting there. This next haiku uses the physical sense of breathlessness after a long climb to evoke awe and wonder in a moment grounded in place.

> catching my breath
> the mountains
> beneath me
> —LINDA PILARSKI

A SENSE OF WHOLENESS, OR HEALING FROM DIVISION

When I feel whole within myself, the divisions within my own psyche are, for that blessed moment, mysteriously reconciled. When I feel whole in relation to others, whatever separates one from the other loses its power to divide, and I feel expansive and connected as a member of a larger body. By linking various times of our lives and communities of our hearts, places have the power to evoke that sense of wholeness, both within ourselves and out in the world.

John, a retired minister, included on his list of sacred places "a pew in the balcony of Wausau's Presbyterian Church, where I first experienced the physical pleasure of a surrounding and holding love unattached to any words or liturgies." This sense of inner wholeness is balanced in the outer world by another of John's entries: "The mostly unused 'Ye Old Yellow Meeting House' near Imlaystown, New Jersey, built in the early eighteenth century, has a sense inside of all the people who had been singing and seeking in this place for centuries."

> By linking various times of our lives and communities of our hearts, places have the power to evoke a sense of wholeness, both within ourselves and out in the world.

The poet Karma Tenzing Wangchuk included in his list places that connected him to other poets whose work he loved, including City Lights Books, where he once ran into Lawrence Ferlinghetti, and the Anza-Borrego Desert of Southern California, a place he knew well and the location of many desert poems by the haiku poet Foster Jewell.

Perhaps the most powerful feelings of sacred wholeness are born straight out of very difficult division, such as a death or a conflict that rends a community or nation. A number of lists included cemeteries where loved ones were buried, and of all the national memorials mentioned, the Vietnam Memorial and the Lincoln Memorial, each connected to wars that deeply divided the nation, were named more often than any others. Arlington National Cemetery was named by three people, including Judith, who said that it was sacred to her individually as well as nationally, explaining, "Both my parents buried there, a beloved

> Perhaps the most powerful feelings of sacred wholeness are born straight out of very difficult division.

cat—(long story), and my sister's ashes scattered near my parents' gravesite."

In the replies I received from members of my own church, St. Paul's, I was surprised and touched that our labyrinth courtyard, the Courtyard of All Souls, was specifically mentioned almost as many times as the church building itself. I was surprised because the courtyard had been in place for only five years when I sent out my survey, just a baby's breath in church years. I was touched because I had helped build it. The courtyard is made of sand-set pavers laid out in the pattern of a labyrinth. The center of the labyrinth is a mosaic of gray, black, white, and red stones collected from

> A haiku grounded in place can reach out and share the ties that connect us to the earth, and through the earth, to each other.

local beaches and embedded in mortar. It was planned and installed during a period of painful internal division in the parish, known to those who lived through it as "The Troubles."

One recent sunny June afternoon, members of St. Paul's Women's Spiritual Growth Group met in the courtyard to write haiku in honor of the five-year anniversary of the courtyard dedication. We started by reading aloud a verse from Isaiah that had provided inspiration to the courtyard committee during its planning phase.

> I will lead the blind by a road they do not know, by paths they have not known I will guide them. I will turn the darkness before them into light, the rough places into level ground. These are the things I will do, and I will not forsake them.
>
> —Isaiah 42:16

Then we talked about the courtyard's history, looked at pictures of the installation, and wrote some haiku.

Sue, a member of the committee that proposed, designed, and raised money for the courtyard—and also a member of the parish vestry throughout the time of "The Troubles"—wrote this poem for the Courtyard of All Souls.

> many hands
> warm, cold stones together
> breathing room
> —Sue Taylor

In our conversations before starting to write, Kate said she liked how the beach stones in the center acquired their polished appearance—by tumbling about in sand. Then she wrote this poem, which includes a reference to the Isaiah passage.

> red ocean stones
> rough places made level
> circles of love
> —Kate Spear

Like most everyone who was part of the parish when the courtyard was installed, my own memories of that time are mixed. They include pain and division right alongside deep pride and communion. Here is a haiku I wrote for that time and place, while watching the afternoon shadows move across the courtyard five years later.

> sun and shade play
> across turns in the path—
> the Courtyard of All Souls
> —M.D.M.

A few weeks after these poems were written, they were included as part of the closing blessing at a Sunday service held out in the courtyard. We stood together on the circling paths, blessing each other and all the stones—warm and cold, rough and smooth, in light and in shadow.

Our connections to the important places of our lives are deeply personal, based on unique experiences and relationships. At the same time, the feelings that bind us to those places can be shared and understood by most everyone because they are tied to universal human experiences and longings—to the comfort of home, the wonder and awe of creation, the sense of wholeness and healing. A haiku grounded in place can reach out and share the ties that connect us to the earth, and through the earth, to each other.

Practice: Seasons of Life

What are the *kigo* of your life—the seasonal words with special resonance for you?

This practice will help spark memories and associations in developing your own personal list of *kigo* to use in your haiku. These are the seasonal elements that connect the passing years together, linking all the seasons of life. Because they come from your unique experience, the elements on your list will be different from anyone else's. However, because we all share the hopes, sorrows, and joys of the common human spirit, a haiku with your *kigo* can reach out and touch others' feelings and spirits, as well as your own.

You will need paper and pencil, and at least twenty minutes of quiet time. Give yourself the time you need. *(If you are doing this practice in a group, you will want additional time to share your results with each other.)*

- First, look over the whole practice; then go through the steps one by one.
- Start with a grid using these six headings: **Daily Life, Plants, Animals, Sun-Moon-Stars, Earth,** and **Weather**

and Length of Days. You can either use the grid below or draw your own on a fresh piece of paper. Allow enough room under each heading for several phrases or more. Title your grid with the name of the current season. (If you live in a climate that does not have distinct seasons, then write the name of the current month.)

Current Season

Daily Life (social events, holidays)	Plants (in nature and for food)
Animals (in nature and for food)	Sun-Moon-Stars
Earth (mountains, lakes, rivers, the sea, forests)	Weather and Length of Days

- If it is practical, go outside and find a place to sit comfortably. If that's not practical, get comfortable where you are.
- Relax, breathe, and sink into the realm of the current season, both as it is for you in memory and as it is

today. What words and images come to mind? Use the grid to spark associations, then write them in their categories.

Tip: Look for associations that are personal to you. For example, winter and Christmas go together for many people who live in the northern hemisphere. However, rather than writing "Christmas" under the **Daily Life** heading, think about your favorite Christmas food or family traditions, and enter those specifics under the categories they fit best.

- Keep going until you have at least one or two items under each category. *(If you are doing this practice in a group, this would be a good time to share kigo among the group. If you have the means, write the headings where everyone can see them. Under each heading, write down two or three seasonal references from those who are comfortable sharing.)*
- Using this material as a resource, write a seasonal haiku. Include in your haiku an image from right now (this passing moment) along with an image that you associate with the season in a timeless way.
- Finished? Take a moment to enjoy what you've written. Congratulations on your haiku! *(If you are doing this exercise in a group, give all the group members a chance to share their haiku if they choose.)*

Looking over your lists of personal seasonal references, do you see elements that you would set apart and call sacred? These might be elements that touch you in a place of deep peace, or that give you a sense of belonging in the world. When you look at the headings from that point of view, what additional *kigo* can you add to each category?

In the coming week, develop a list of places that are sacred to you—places where you feel at home, in awe, or whole and healed. Include places both inside and outside your community. Consider making a mini-pilgrimage to each place within your community, writing a haiku at each location. For those places outside your community—think about taking a haiku trip!

CHAPTER FIVE

Inspired Conversations

I also am mortal, like everyone else,
a descendant of the first-formed child of earth;
and in the womb of a mother I was molded into flesh,
within the period of ten months, compacted with blood,
from the seed of a man and the pleasure of marriage.
And when I was born, I began to breathe the common air,
and fell upon the kindred earth;
my first sound was a cry, as is true of all.
I was nursed with care in swaddling cloths.
For no king has had a different beginning of existence;
there is for all one entrance into life, and one way out.
—Wisdom of Solomon 7:1–6

> *First, give up being*
> *first. First, come out of the womb.*
> *First breathe, then cry out.*
> *—M.D.M.*

In his later years, the poet Bashō set out on walking journeys throughout Japan. He was drawn to visit places dear to his heart, some of which were known to him only through the poetry of those who came before him. He wanted to share in the experiences that inspired the work he loved; he longed to "feel the truth of old poems." Along the way, Bashō wrote new poems, picking up images and themes from old ones that moved him deeply, carrying them forward in the experiences of his own life. In this way, Bashō entered into conversation with bygone poets and the larger human spirit, leaving a record of the exchanges for those who follow on the road.

Pilgrimages—trips to places where significant events happened that create identity and bring meaning to life—are a central practice in many faith traditions. In pilgrimage, the conversation with those who came before takes on a physical as well as a spiritual dimension, uniting body and mind to address the whole person. For those who cannot go on pilgrimage—or those between pilgrimages—encounters with sacred texts also integrate mind, heart, and senses.

In one such practice, Jewish rabbis and their disciples chant memorized verses of scripture in a form of prayerful meditation called *haga*. Practiced over many generations, *haga* turns an encounter with scripture into an experience that involves all the elements of the self, so that the word of God becomes more fully present in life.

In the early years of Christianity, the desert ascetics carried *haga* forward in a practice that came to be called *lectio divina,* meaning "holy or sacred reading." Because it was not realistic in those times for each individual to own a complete set of scripture, these desert mothers and fathers would gather together to hear the word of God read aloud as a communal practice. After a group reading, they would memorize the verses and take them back to their cells for further meditation and prayer. Over the centuries, the practice of *lectio divina* came to include a prayerful response to the passage at hand, holding up to God concerns and events of the current day

haga: a prayerful Jewish meditation of chanted scripture

in the context of the day's readings. In this way, those who practiced *lectio divina* took part in a running conversation with the Spirit that had been ongoing since the ancient texts were first composed.

Widely practiced in the early Christian church, *lectio divina* is a way of experiencing God's presence in scripture. The process involves reading a passage aloud slowly and prayerfully, focusing on words and phrases that resonate in the heart at the moment of reading. The reader "ruminates" on these words, chewing them over and letting them find voice through personal memory and immediate concerns. Then the reader listens for God's voice and uses the language of the passage in prayer.

Because *lectio divina* is not concerned with analyzing scripture, but with responding to it from deep within through repeated readings, it leads into an encounter with texts that is active, immediate, and engaged. And because of its focus on language, *lectio divina* is a great companion for writing haiku. I was introduced to *lectio divina* at about the same time haiku entered my life, and the two fell together in my spiritual practice almost as if each had just been waiting for the other to show up.

> *lectio divina:* holy or sacred reading of scripture not concerned with analyzing the text, but with responding to it from deep within through repeated readings

After being raised in the Protestant Church and leaving it behind as a young adult, I had returned in my middle years to a new relationship with the Christian faith, and it was a time of great change and renewal in my spiritual life. I began to use the steps of *lectio divina* to write 5-7-5 verse in response to scripture passages, copying my response onto a little yellow sticky note and putting it next to the passage in my Bible. Gradually, my Bible filled with sticky notes of short verse—commentary, argument, sometimes prayer.

Some contained haiku-like imagery. Others, such as the poem "First, give up being" at the beginning of this chapter, were more like advice to myself than like any conventional haiku. Some could hardly be called poems at all. Still, I structured them in three lines of seventeen syllables and tried to include one or more words from the passage itself. The discipline of working within a form nudged me deeper into the passages than I would otherwise have gone, and writing the poems was fun.

"Feel the truth of old poems."
—Bashō

The steps of *lectio divina* can inspire haiku in response to all kinds of writing, whether scripture passages, texts from faith traditions, or any poem or piece of writing that moves you deeply. By connecting words in the text to the experience of your own life and writing a poetic response, you join with Bashō in his quest to "feel the truth of old poems."

A pilgrimage is travel for transformation

Journeying to a sacred place for the purpose of enlightenment, to fulfill a vow or religious requirement, or as part of a spiritual discipline is one of the oldest forms of religious practice. The ancient Hindu tradition of visiting *tīrthas,* or holy sites on the banks of sacred waters, reaches far back into antiquity and remains a central feature of religious life in India today. In the spiritual sense, a *tīrtha,* such as the River Ganges, can be seen as a ford or place of crossing between the human world and the divine world. Bathing in its waters is a way for pilgrims to purify themselves and come into contact with the realm of heaven.

The largest annual pilgrimage in the world today is the hajj, the journey to Mecca made by Muslims during the month of Dhu al-Hijja, the last month of the Islamic year. Every year, the hajj serves as an expression of unity for the far-flung Muslim faith, bringing together millions of believers from all over the world to meet and worship together as one.

For haiku poets, the tradition of making pilgrimages to poetic places and writing new poems at the site is still going strong, except that today these places are situated all over the world. One of the oldest sites is at the Royal Botanic Gardens, Kew, in London, where a haiku by the Japanese poet Takahama Kyoshi, written after a visit to the gardens, is carved in a haiku stone. On the other side of the globe, in New Zealand, Katikati's Haiku Pathway, a meandering footpath alongside the Uretara Stream, contains the largest collection of haiku stones outside Japan, with haiku written by New Zealanders and by poets from around the world who have visited the site.

A Joint Venture between *Lectio Divina* and Writing Haiku

The best introduction to *lectio divina* is doing it, so let's get started. The next few pages contain an instructional guide using the steps of *lectio divina* to write haiku. You might want to read over the steps first, just to see what lies ahead. Then give yourself the gift of a real-time, mind-and-body experience with the Spirit, in company with the words of someone who has traveled this road before you.

You will need a quiet place where you can read aloud, a comfortable chair, paper and pencil for writing, and some time to yourself—at least twenty minutes or so. You will also need a text to focus on for your practice. Choose a favorite scripture passage, a poem you particularly like, or any text that calls to you and that you would like to delve into deeper. Keep the passage fairly short—about a paragraph in length.

If you like, you can practice with this passage from the book of Matthew:

You are the salt of the earth; but if salt has lost its taste, how can its saltiness be restored? It is no longer good for anything, but is thrown out and trampled under foot. You are the light of the world. A city built on a hill cannot be hid. No one after lighting a lamp puts it under the bushel basket, but on the lampstand, and it gives light to all in the house. In the same way, let your light shine before others, so that they may see your good works and give glory to your Father in heaven.

—MATTHEW 5:13–16

Traditionally, *lectio divina* has four steps:

- *lectio* (reading and listening)
- *meditatio* (meditation)
- *oratio* (prayer)
- *contemplatio* (contemplation)

We will take each step in turn. Be patient along the way. Do not rush ahead to writing haiku. Instead, allow the process to do its work, so that you can fully experience the journey.

LECTIO (READING AND LISTENING)

The first step of *lectio divina* involves both reading and listening. Listening is not really possible until you fall silent, so get comfortable and spend a few moments in quiet. Focus your attention on the moment at hand: your breathing, the touch of air on your skin. Do not worry if your thoughts wander a bit. Just watch them, wherever they go. Acknowledge the presence of the Creative Spirit that lives in all things. Prepare to listen with an open heart.

Now slowly read the passage you have selected. If it's practical where you are, read the passage out loud.

Spend another moment in silence, then read the passage aloud again. Throughout the reading, listen for words or phrases that seem to rise up and call to you right now. These words might appear in sharper focus on the page, or they might actually seem to "rise up" from the paper. You might have the sense that the passage opens up to you through a particular word or phrase.

On a separate sheet of paper, jot down any words or phrases that call to you at this moment.

Be open to all the words that come to you—those with warm and positive energy, as well as those that carry negative energy. For example, in the passage from Matthew above, the phrase "thrown out and trampled under foot" jumps out at me. It would be easy to skip over those words, not expecting (or wanting) to receive anything of value from them. But this is not the stage of the process to pick and choose. Include any word or phrase that resonates, whether its tone is sweet or harsh.

> A central aspect of the practice of listening is to set aside our expectations and assumptions as much as possible. Then we can see the potential in each moment for something new to be revealed.... When we listen with our heart, we listen with love that is rooted in gratitude and appreciation. Everyone and everything speaks to us of God.
> —CHRISTINE VALTERS PAINTNER
> AND SR. LUCY WYNKOOP, OSB

Continue reading the passage over, until you have collected all its words and phrases that speak to you now.

MEDITATIO (MEDITATION)

Set the original passage aside for the moment and turn your attention to your list of words and phrases. In silence, ruminate on these words. If one word or phrase stands out in particular, repeat it over to yourself out loud, until you have committed it to memory.

While meditating, give these words space to interact with your current thoughts, memories, hopes, and dreams. If a memory is sparked, jot it down. Some of the words might stir your senses. For example, the word *salt* in the passage from Matthew brings particular foods to my mind, and the foods bring memories with them. In your meditations, what are you hearing, tasting, smelling, seeing, feeling? Especially note any images that come to you: pictures in your mind's eye of people, places, or things.

> Give these words space to interact with your current thoughts, memories, hopes, and dreams.

Relax, keep the door open, and let it all in. Allow the words and phrases from the passage to speak to you through your own experiences and feelings.

ORATIO (PRAYER)

Now is the time to respond. If it feels right, you might start by writing or saying a short prayer. Offer up your concerns, hopes, and intentions for this day, using some of the language of the passage in your prayer.

Then write a haiku in response to the passage. Include in your haiku a word or short phrase that called to you from the passage. It is okay to use a different form of a word, if it works better in your haiku. For example, if you chose the word *salt,* it is okay to use *salty* or *salted* in your haiku. Also, if it feels right, include an image from your meditation jottings in your haiku.

> The idea is not to analyze or explain the passage, but to enter into it through your own experience and feelings.

Think of your haiku as part of a conversation. The idea is not to analyze or explain the passage, but to enter into it through your own experience and feelings. Open up to its truth, and look for the relationship between its truth and the truth of your own life. Even if your haiku is not "about" the passage at all, the spirit of the passage will be present in what you write.

Read your haiku out loud; then read the passage one more time.

Here are three very different poems, each composed from a session of *lectio divina* with the example passage from Matthew 5, "You are the salt of the earth.... You are the light of the world...."

> Resting on the sofa
> warm sun soaking into me ...
> light restored
> —SUE TAYLOR

> darkness
> flashlight's beam
> welcoming
> —KATE SPEAR

> trampled underfoot
> I am the light of the world—
> What's it to be?
> —VAL JOHNSTONE

CONTEMPLATIO (CONTEMPLATION)

Finally, let go of all the words, and rest in the place that holds no words. Return to silence and rest in the presence of God.

How did it go? Did your feelings about the passage change while you were writing your haiku?

Like other types of meditation, the benefits of *lectio divina* expand and deepen with continued practice. So do the benefits of writing haiku. You might return to the same passage more than once, or you might choose a new passage at each session. When I write haiku in *lectio divina,* I make a copy of the haiku on a sticky note or bookmark and keep it with the original text. That way, if I return to the passage and read it again at a later date, I can pick up the threads of the earlier poetic conversation and carry it forward from wherever I am now. Practiced regularly, *lectio divina* and writing haiku may deepen your relationship with the texts and the Spirit that lives within them.

Taking the Conversation Out into the World

The practice of *lectio divina* was an integral part of monastic life for centuries before the four steps were defined and formally written down. When the early desert mothers and fathers practiced holy or sacred reading, they may not have used a multistep process at all. Because memorization was an important part of their practice, they would carry the verses with them internally throughout the day. In their prayers and ruminations, they would seek to integrate the words of scripture with all parts of their life.

The power of this basic approach has not changed in the passing of a couple of thousand years. When you carry the words of sacred texts out into the world with you, and look with attention, you may see the words reflected back to you in the common events and objects of daily life. If you use those events and objects in your haiku, you can enter into conversation with the Creative Spirit wherever you go. As an example, consider how Annika Wallendahl approached writing haiku for a collection of Lenten reflections for my home parish of St. Paul's.

Annika is an environmental manager who has also written for a living, so you might think that one short meditation on a passage of scripture would be a snap for her. And yet, after she agreed to take one on, the words did not come easily.

"I kept getting stuck," Annika recounted. "I had to come back to the scripture over and over. How could I make it relevant to me? I get so wrapped up in day-to-day things that I sometimes forget to turn to scripture or prayer. I wanted a reminder—like little road markers—that would help me remember scripture throughout the day. I decided to tie the readings to things I see all the time. That worked for me. I wanted my responses to be short, concrete, and literal, which fits with haiku. So then I asked myself, what do I see?"

The following two haiku from Annika's Lenten reflection are each set at a local place, familiar to most people who live in my community. They show events that could happen on most any day in early spring. As you will see from her comments after each poem, Annika does not view these haiku as literal interpretations of the Bible verses. They are simply what she saw when she looked around her and paid attention.

> But the jar he was making did not turn out as he had hoped, so the potter squashed the jar into a lump of clay and started again.
>
> —JEREMIAH 18:4

> Crooked sand castle
> leveled by a little girl.
> Shipping boats inch along the Straits.
>
> —ANNIKA WALLENDAHL

Annika: "If you make a mistake, you can start all over again, like building sand castles."

> But you are not controlled by your sinful nature. You are controlled by the Spirit if you have the Spirit of God living in you.
>
> —ROMANS 8:9

> Apricot dog dashes at
> cars on Rhody Drive—
> Invisible Fence keeps him safe.
>
> —ANNIKA WALLENDAHL

Annika: "I feel like I have an invisible fence that keeps me out of harm's way."

Because the words of scripture are thousands of years old and encrusted with centuries of interpretation, it can be hard to remember that they were written by ordinary human beings, people who encountered God in their lives and wanted to tell others about it. When you carry their words out into *your* world, the "old poets" have the chance to share their experiences with you in the context of your own life. Writing your haiku response, you join your experiences with theirs, walking and talking in the company of a sympathetic and understanding friend.

The Mushroom on the Fence Post

the old fence post
sprouts a mushroom cap
I WILL BE WHAT I WILL BE
—M.D.M.

Sometimes I go looking for God's Spirit in the world around me, and sometimes it seems as if the Spirit comes looking for me. That was how it felt when I saw the mushroom growing out of the old fence post.

When you carry the words of sacred texts out into the world with you, and look with attention, you may see the words reflected back to you in the common events and objects of daily life.

Every morning before breakfast, I walk through the woods that surround our home. Part of my path follows a fence line our neighbor set up many years before we moved here. Season by season, the rough-hewn fence posts take on greater life, as tiny seeds and spores find their homes in the old wood's cracks and knotholes. One summer a small purple mushroom sprang out of a post's lichen-covered top. The mushroom stuck around for days, and I grew quite fond of it over many morning meetings. Finally, remembering that nothing lasts forever, I carried my camera out with me and took a few snapshots. One of the photos turned out pretty well, so I ordered an enlargement for framing. By the time the print came back from the shop, the mushroom was long gone from our neighbor's fence post. I was happy to see my friend again up close in the photograph.

Then I noticed that, in the enlargement, a tiny white dot on the mushroom's crown had taken hazy shape. I peered at the photo, blinked, and looked closer. Another mushroom, nearly microscopic in size, was growing directly out of the purple mushroom's cap.

When I showed the picture to my spiritual director and pointed out the tiny umbrella shape, she exclaimed with delight, "Wonderful! A virgin birth!"

> Sometimes I go looking for God's Spirit in the world around me, and sometimes it seems as if the Spirit comes looking for me.

Now, I really like the idea of the parthenogenetic mushroom on my neighbor's fence post reflecting back an image of the Madonna and Child. But when I first saw the purple mushroom sprouting from its bed of lichen and moss, what came to mind was not a scene from Luke's Gospel or any book in the New Testament. Instead, I was reminded of one of my favorite passages in all of scripture: the encounter between Moses and God at the burning bush.

> But Moses said to God, "If I come to the Israelites and say to them, 'The God of your ancestors has sent me to you,' and they ask me, 'What is his name?' what shall I say to them?" God said to Moses, "I AM WHO I AM." He said further, "Thus you shall say to the Israelites, 'I AM has sent me to you.'"
>
> —EXODUS 3:13–14

What a great scene in an even greater story. I like it that the meeting between God and Moses started when Moses turned aside to investigate an unexpected sight in the natural world. I like the way

Moses argued with God, twisting and turning in one desperate attempt after another to get out of his great and overwhelming task. I like the way God met him at every turn. And I especially like God's answer when Moses asked, "What is your name?"

In the Bible, names are more than mere labels; they have meaning and power. They bestow identity and say something about the bearer's essential nature. In this way, they *define* the person who bears the name.

But God's answer to Moses is no definition. Instead, it is an early form of the Hebrew word *to be,* which can be translated, "I am who I am," "I am what I am," or, "I will be what I will be." The translation is commonly printed in small caps in Bibles, to set it off from the rest of the text.

Those words tell me that God is not constrained by definition or expectation—not mine, and not my church's. God will not be constrained even by God's own words. Strangely, this enigmatic answer makes me feel light and alive. It makes me feel that I am not constrained by definition either. The mushroom growing out of the fence post, in some way, embodied that for me, and I wanted to acknowledge and respond to it in the words of a haiku. The poem that starts this section, "the old fence post," captures my first feeling about the mushroom, when I encountered it on my morning walks. This next poem contains the surprising image revealed in the photograph, and ends with the same expansive last line.

> God is not constrained by definition or expectation.... God will not be constrained even by God's own words.

mushroom caps mushroom
on the old fence post
I WILL BE WHAT I WILL BE

—M.D.M.

Lichen and moss growing willy-nilly from a rotting fence post, topped by a small purple mushroom, topped by another tiny mushroom—the very image of abundant life and the spirit of surprise in unfolding creation. For me, the mushroom on the fence post was one of those little "road markers" that Annika described—a bit of scripture alive in my own backyard.

Practice: *Lectio* + Haiku

The practice of *lectio divina* draws the wisdom in sacred texts into everyday life. Writing a haiku is a creative response to what you meet, moment by moment, on the path of life.

This practice provides a number of short scripture passages with themes of "creation" or "life's path" to choose from, with directions on how to use the steps of *lectio divina* to write haiku in response. If you've already practiced these *lectio divina* steps with the Matthew passage in this chapter, you'll have a good foundation for this. If you haven't had the time to "pre-practice," you might want to refer back to the chapter text at each step for further clarification.

You will need paper and pencil, and at least twenty minutes of quiet time. Give yourself the time you need. *(If you are doing this practice in a group, you will want additional time to share your results with each other.)*

- First, look over the whole practice; then go through the steps one by one.
- Wherever you are, relax, breathe, and look around.
- Read over the following scripture passages and choose one to focus on for this practice.

I will lead the blind by a road they do not know,
by paths they have not known I will guide them.
I will turn the darkness before them into light,

the rough places into level ground.
These are the things I will do, and I will not forsake
them.

—Isaiah 42:16

A highway shall be there, and it shall be called the
Holy Way … it shall be for God's people; no traveler,
not even fools, shall go astray.

—Isaiah 35:8

You show me the path of life. In your presence there
is fullness of joy, in your right hand are pleasures
forevermore.

—Psalm 16:11

Blessed are those … who have set their hearts on
pilgrimage.

—Psalm 84:5

Yours is the day, yours also the night;
you established the luminaries and the sun.
You have fixed all the bounds of the earth;
you made summer and winter.

—Psalm 74:16–17

The one who made the Pleiades and Orion, and
turns deep darkness into the morning, and darkens
the day into night, who calls for the waters of the sea,
and pours them out on the surface of the earth, the
Lord is his name.

—Amos 5:8

Send out your bread upon the waters, for after many
days you will get it back…. Just as you do not know
how the breath comes to the bones in the mother's
womb, so you do not know the work of God, who
makes everything.

—Ecclesiastes 11:1, 5

Be still and know that I am God.

—*Psalm 46:10*

Lectio

- After choosing one of these passages for your practice, take a moment in silence, becoming aware of God's presence.
- Slowly read the passage, then read it again, listening with both heart and mind. If it is practical where you are, do the readings out loud. *(If you are doing this practice in a group, ask for a volunteer to read the passage out loud to the group; then, after a few moments of silence, ask for a different volunteer to read it aloud. If your group includes both women and men, it can be helpful to hear the passage in the voice of both a man and a woman.)*
- Jot down a few words or phrases from the text that "rise up" and carry energy for you at this moment.

Meditatio

- Now put the passage aside and turn to the words you jotted down. Spend time with the memories, feelings, and associations they carry to you.

Oratio

- Write a haiku that includes at least one of those words. (It's okay to use a different form of the word if it works better in your haiku. For example, if the word *light* is on your list, it's okay to use *lighting*.)
- Read your haiku (aloud, if practical), then return to the passage and read it one more time. *(If you are doing this exercise in a group, give all the group members a chance to share their haiku, if they choose.)*

Contemplatio

- Take another moment to be silent in God's presence.
- In the coming week, carry a passage with you wherever you go. You can choose one of the passages from the list above or choose a short passage from another text that holds meaning for you. Repeat the passage over to yourself until you have it memorized. Then, throughout the week, look for "road markers" that reflect its words or message back to you. Use those moments on the path as inspiration for new haiku.

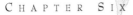

Haiku in Community

letting go
of a slanderous heart—
while shelling beans
        —Hosai Ozaki (1885–1926)

Thinking back on the family and church potlucks of my Ohio childhood, I remember the deviled eggs above all else. I can see them now, laid out in concentric circles on decorative platters and in rows on shallow serving dishes. During the summer, when eggs were cheap, the white-and-gold offerings might cover half of a long folding table.

My mother's were, of course, the best. But, having grown up with them, I *knew* my mother's deviled eggs. By my mid-teens, I might have even made the eggs we brought to the picnic myself, arranging them on our cut-glass platter while Mom put together the potato salad. So, though it took an effort of will, I eschewed the McGee family deviled eggs at potlucks, and instead sampled every other egg I could get my hands on before the laden dishes had nothing left on them but a few sprigs of decorative parsley.

Oh, the wealth of ways to make deviled eggs! Such glorious variety, each to be devoured in a series of two quick bites. Red paprika or chopped chives sprinkled on top: these were ideas I could quickly grasp. But a beanie of pimento-stuffed olive? Here was a strange and exotic approach, deserving more than a single taste. One recipe with sweet pickle relish stirred into the stuffing, another without. One with an abundance of mustard, another with just a dab. Perhaps one plate of halved eggs stuffed with a mixture that, bizarrely, contained no mustard at all.

And then there was curry. When I was ten, I might not have finished a deviled egg with curry spices in it, but today I would.

The glorious variety of human creativity in small things can also be tasted in haiku written in a group setting. When those who "cook" haiku join together for companionship and find inspiration in a common theme, the result is a unique combination of flavors that no one could have created alone.

> When those who "cook" haiku join together for companionship and find inspiration in a common theme, the result is a unique combination of flavors that no one could have created alone.

Poetry is not the only thing that comes into being at such a gathering. If you have ever joined with others to create something new—a meal, a quilt, a theatrical play, a community garden, a house, a barn—then you know that in addition to what is made in the outer world, a new set of relationships comes out of the shared creation. I may not always be able to let go of a "slanderous heart" while shelling beans for the big picnic at the county fair, but it is a pretty good place to start. In the process of creative work together, new bonds are formed, and old ones deepened or transformed.

Writing a haiku on your own is a way to record and share the deep feeling of a moment; doing it with others is a way to both create and nurture community. Not only that, but writing haiku as a group experience can be flat-out fun.

To show you what I mean, let me introduce Sheikh Jamal Rahman and the Blush of the Beloved group at the Interfaith Community Church in Seattle.

Every Particle in the World Is a Mirror

On a beautiful blue-sky Saturday in winter, in an odd-shaped room of a century-old house of worship, ten of us join together in a session of reading deeply into sacred poetry and responding with sacred poetry of our own.

The place is the Interfaith Community Church in the Ballard neighborhood of Seattle. Sheikh Jamal Rahman, the Muslim Sufi minister who serves as cominister at the church, has invited me to give a haiku-writing workshop in the afternoon session of his Blush of the Beloved class, which meets here every Saturday.

When I arrive shortly before noon, the class is already deep into its morning session. Jamal greets me warmly and invites me to join them. I sit quietly and observe an ongoing conversation about approaches to meditation, openness to meditation, resistance to meditation, and acceptance of resistance to meditation. I am impressed by the caring that people in the room show to each other. At noon, we move to the lower floor of the old church and share a vegetarian meal of soup, bread, and fruit.

Listen for the words or phrases that speak to you today in a personal way, the words that "rise up" with special energy.

After lunch, back in the odd-shaped room, I begin the haiku workshop with a few moments of silence. Then I ask each person around the circle to "say your name, then identify *one thing* that is sacred to you—one thing that gives life meaning and wholeness, or holiness." Because I know it can be tempting to generalize, and challenging to focus on the particulars that find a good home in haiku, I ask that they identify something real, specific, and personal. Not the big rhetorical truth, but a small truth about their own life. Not peace (though peace is certainly sacred), but one thing that brings them peace. Not nature, but one object or spot in nature where they find joy and wholeness.

To set the tone, I go first. "My name is Margaret. My husband, David, and I share our lives with a small black dog named Bingo. Bingo is one of the things that gives my life meaning and wholeness. Bingo is sacred to me."

Jamal, seated to my left, goes next. After saying his name, he opens his hands and says that this room is sacred to him, with its beautiful objects and the beautiful people he meets here. I look around me. The room is a comfortable size for our group, not too big or too small. Its floor is scattered with a hodgepodge of chairs, cushions, small tables, and plants. At the far end, wooden cupboards fill the space beneath a pair of clear windows. The pale lavender walls are hung with kids' pictures, along with other artwork that evokes the Divine from different cultures and points of view. Between and among the wall hangings, I have taped up big sheets of white paper to use in the workshop. Although this room is certainly bigger than Bingo, it is still specific, personal, concrete, and immediate. After all, we are right here in it. I have the sense of being in a space that has soaked up a lot of prayer over a lot of years.

> The goal is to entice every individual in the room into the process, and not to intimidate a single one out of it.

We continue around the circle. Sacred things, big and small, are offered, including a variety of places and objects from the natural world. After the last person in the circle has spoken, I explain to the group that, in leading up to writing haiku, we will follow a process based on the steps of *lectio divina,* a prayerful practice of reading scripture developed in monasteries centuries ago. I tell them that *lectio divina* is not concerned with analyzing a text, but with responding to it from deep within, through repeated readings. Beyond that, I am not going to talk about *lectio divina* or explain its steps. We are just going to do it.

I hand out copies of our text, "Every Particle in the World Is a Mirror," by Mahmud Shabistari. Then I read the poem aloud, slowly.

EVERY PARTICLE IN THE WORLD IS A MIRROR

Every particle of the world is a mirror,
In each atom lies the blazing light
    of a thousand suns.
Cleave the heart of a rain-drop,
    a hundred pure oceans will flow forth.
Look closely at a grain of sand,
    the seed of a thousand beings can be seen.
The foot of an ant is larger than an elephant;
In essence, a drop of water
    is no different than the Nile.
In the heart of a barley-corn
    lies the fruit of a hundred harvests;
Within the pulp of a millet seed
    an entire universe can be found.
In the wing of a fly, an ocean of wonder;
    In the pupil of the eye, an endless heaven.
Though the inner chamber of the heart is small,
    the Lord of both worlds
    gladly makes a home there.
          —MAHMUD SHABISTARI (1288–1340)

After a moment's silence, I ask Jamal to read it out loud again, so that we can hear the words in a different voice. Before he begins, I tell the group, "Listen for the words or phrases that speak to you today in a personal way, the words that 'rise up' with special energy," and I suggest that they circle the words on the page or jot them down on a separate sheet of paper. I remind them to include words with negative as well as positive energy.

After Jamal's reading, I ask the group to tell me the words they highlighted. *"Wonder,"* someone calls out, and another says, *"mirror."* I write them on one of the big pieces of paper that I have taped up on the walls. The words come pouring out: *cleave, atom, elephant, Nile, ruby, a grain of sand, home,* and *heart.* I keep writing, and they keep calling out words, until everyone has added their words to the list.

This completes the *lectio* step of the process. It is time to move on to *meditatio.*

I tell the group members to choose just one or two items from the list, and then to ruminate on those words, spending time, allowing the words to connect to their own memories, experiences, hopes, and dreams, and jotting down memories and images that rise up from these words.

After five or ten minutes of silent scribbling, I ask if anyone would like to share one or two images. Su, who has actually been to the Nile, says, "The Nile, becoming larger, and thinner, and black earth. I want the knowledge of the Nile." Someone says, "A place of buoyancy," and someone else says, "Holding a heart in my hand." Another voice offers, "Watery brown compassionate eyes," and another, "To understand a grain of sand while holding it in the palm of my hand." "Wonder of wonders—astonishing!" says Jamal.

For me, writing in a group always becomes a challenging exercise in turning off my inner critic and accepting what is on the page.

I write the phrases and images up where everyone can see them.

After a big sheet of paper is full of material, we are ready to leave *meditatio* and go on to *oratio.*

I hand out a one-page introduction to the haiku verse. It gives a brief description of the essentials of the form, along with four examples written by haiku masters—two translations from the classics and two modern English haiku. I read the description out loud, then ask different group members to read the example haiku out loud. One of the examples contains seventeen syllables divided into 5-7-5 lines. Another example contains eleven syllables, divided into stressed lines of 2-3-2 stresses or beats. The others do not follow that kind of structure. All four show close attention to a passing moment, and all four contain sharp images that evoke feeling in the moment. After each example, I point out some of the ways it illustrates what goes into a haiku. We are finished with the introduction to the haiku form in about five minutes.

> Each haiku is a surprise, a unique creation from an individual imagination.

Next, I choose two images from the list that the class has produced and put them together in three lines, rearranging some of the words and writing the three lines up where all can see them. After a couple of suggestions from the room, we have something like this:

> in my open palm
> I hold one grain of sand …
> a place of buoyancy

Voilà—a haiku.

The result is not a particularly great poem, and I am not at all sure what it means. But that is okay. Many people feel anxious about being "creative" in front of others. I know this is true because I am one of those anxious people. The goal at this stage is to entice every individual in the room into the process, and not to intimidate a single one out of it. So the purpose of the example is simply to show the group's own words coming together, in a matter of moments, to make a three-line poem.

"Now," I say, "here's what we're going to do. You will write your own haiku. Include in your haiku a word from Shabistari's poem. Also, use either a word that came out of our process or another that strikes you now. For material, use the images that came to you while meditating on the words, or an image that comes to you while you are writing. Feel free to use a different form of a word—such as *buoyant* instead of *buoyancy*—if that works better."

I offer two more quick bits of advice. First: short, concrete words are easier to work with than multisyllable, abstract words. Second: a formal structure that involves counting accents or syllables can be helpful, especially if you are new to the form. Just don't get too tied up in it. The important thing is the image.

And we're off.

Minutes tick by. Some class members are counting on their fingers. Others stare into the air. I am trying to write, too, though the lines don't come easily. For me, writing in a group always becomes a challenging exercise in turning off my inner critic and accepting what is on the page.

After about ten minutes, we stop writing and it is time to share. I assure everyone that it is okay to "pass." Sharing is voluntary. Before we begin, I also ask group members to speak slowly and distinctly when reading their poems aloud. That way, the rest of us will have a chance to absorb the words.

We go around the circle. The first few class members are happy to share what they have written. Like deviled eggs at a potluck, every haiku offers flavors quite different from the last, which is perhaps my favorite thing about this exercise. "Every Particle in the World Is a Mirror" gives our work a shared context. Within that context, each haiku is a surprise, a unique creation from an individual imagination.

Jane's haiku transports us to a distant land:

> Standing in the savanna grass,
> soft, compassionate strength,
> the elephants
> —JANE GANAS LONG

Jamal's haiku is all surprise and prayer:

> Wonders within wonders!
> Astonishing!
> Allah be praised!
> —JAMAL RAHMAN

We are halfway around the circle when the turn comes to Sally, who quickly says, "I'm sorry, I'll have to pass." Sally explains that she tried to make her image work in a structure, but she just could not deal with the form.

This can happen, and there is no way of knowing it will unless you try. For some people, counting syllables or beats provides a helpful space for writing haiku. The analytical side of the mind seems to get diverted into the structure, giving the creative side more room to play. For others, the same technique can be a distraction and a trap.

Maria Luiza, the next person in the circle, helps Sally out by saying, "That's okay, I'll read mine, and then you won't pass, because mine isn't much either." As Maria Luiza reads, we again hear a poem quite unlike everyone else's.

> The mirror can show
> as above and so below—
> look, enjoy, then grow.
> —MARIA LUIZA C. RAMOS

My little one-page introduction to the haiku form says nothing about rhyme, and none of my examples contains internal rhymes. Yet here is a seventeen-syllable poem that rhymes at the end of every line. We have received yet another testament to the unquenchable nature of the human creative spirit.

After a moment to enjoy Maria Luiza's poem, I ask Sally if she would be willing to share just her image with us. Experience tells me that the one who is least inclined to speak in a group is not necessarily the one with the least to offer. Although I do not want to put anyone on the spot, I do want our process to be as inclusive as possible. So after assuring Sally that we understand this is not a haiku, I say that we would just enjoy hearing about her image.

She nods, then reads aloud, "I wonder what ruby is contained within this cracked moment." After a brief silence, I ask her to read it again. The way she reads the words, they fall naturally into three lines.

> I wonder
> what ruby is contained
> within this cracked moment.
> —SALLY MARQUIS

After brief silence, I comment that I think she has written a beautiful haiku. Around the room, heads nod. Suddenly, Sally's face opens up in a bright, beaming smile. She pumps her fist in the air, and the room seems to expand around us. No one else passes as we continue around the circle, everyone sharing and listening to haiku.

After all the individual haiku have been read, we join together and write a longer poem together as a group. Every member of the group contributes one haiku verse to the poem. Each verse includes at least two words from "Every Particle in the World Is a Mirror." The chosen words move through the poem, linking one verse to the next. The first and last verses circle around to each other, like the circle of poets. The result is a poem that expresses the individuality of each member of the circle as well as the group as a whole, all within the context of "Every Particle in the World Is a Mirror." (For the steps we used to create this linked-verse poem, see the practice at the end of the chapter.)

BLUSH OF THE BELOVED RESPONDS TO "EVERY PARTICLE IN THE WORLD IS A MIRROR"

> rain-drops
> cleaved, light my   Sally
> way home

> the heart cleaves to the drop
> as the universe—   Jane
> to a star

cleave your wounded heart
allow love a passage in   Andrea
compassion will flow

raindrops!
big, small, splash, plop!   Jamal
ah, how life flows

raindrop finds its way
flows into nourishing pulp   Chris
home sparkles again

seeds open now
in the heart of winter   Margaret
I long for home

damp earth holding seed
until the moment arrives   Rick
—now filled with ripe light

light will fall over
the pulp of seedy sorrow   Pauline
sieving juice to live

I think barley-corn
I then give a laugh to myself   Su
hearty pulp of life

mirror reflects me
I am leaving the beloved home   Maria Luiza
but harvesting the barley-corn

After reading the poem around the circle a couple of times, we are finished with the *oratio* stage of *lectio divina,* and it is time for *contemplatio.* Before finishing up the session, we rest for a few moments of silence.

In discussion and feedback afterward, class members compare the process to dream interpretation or alchemy—a way to get around the analytical mind and find a chink or an opening into the heart. Some say that feelings came easily, and that passing words around the circle for the group poem helped them connect with each other in a new way.

I pack my car with rolls of big paper and sheets of new poems, then take off for home, uplifted by the Spirit in the Blush of the Beloved.

A brief description of haiku to use with groups:

Haiku is a Japanese verse form known for distilling the essence of a moment in time and place through strong nature imagery.

- Most haiku in English consist of three brief, unrhymed lines. When haiku was first written in English, many poets followed a convention of five, seven, and five syllables for each line.
- Today, new English haiku are often shorter, with perhaps two beats or stresses in the first and third lines, and three beats in the second or middle line.
- A successful haiku relies not on exact syllable count, but on close attention to a momentary image and the feeling it evokes, often finding in its essence a link between nature and human nature.

Haiku for Holy Days, Events, and Celebrations

Like deviled eggs made with love and brought to the potluck, haiku written for a special community event can be prepared, brought, and offered for the pleasure of the whole community. The event might be an extended family gathering to celebrate a special birthday of a matriarch or patriarch. It might be the opening of a community space, such as a park or memorial garden. Or it could be a religious occasion—the celebration of a new ministry or a special day in the liturgical calendar. Those who write the haiku have the fun of a creative group experience, and those who hear them read are blessed by the results.

To show you what I mean, let me tell you about the Passover haiku presented at the Bet Shira Congregation's community Seder in Port Townsend, Washington, as part of their annual celebration of freedom and new birth.

I arrive for the Seder a little early to check in with the host and my fellow poets. The Bet Shira Congregation holds their prayer services in the fellowship hall of St. Paul's Episcopal Church, my home parish. Their community Seder is being held there tonight as well, so the venue is familiar to me—a place where I have eaten many a deviled egg over the years. As other early-comers arrive, I see an enticing array of covered dishes pass through the swinging doors into the kitchen. The room slowly fills with chattering friends.

The process is a way to get around the analytical mind and find a chink or an opening into the heart.

And yet, looking around, it seems more like the setting for a wedding reception than a church social. The large round tables are covered in white linen tablecloths. Flowers, candles, and attractive place settings brighten the big room.

On each table, a plate covered in white cloth holds pieces of matzah, or unleavened bread. Another plate with cupped indentations displays a circle of special symbolic foods. There are pitchers of water and bottles of kosher red wine and grape juice. At the head table, two extra empty goblets complete the picture.

The table settings are not the only clues that tonight will be different from all other nights. Something in the atmosphere—a sense of anticipation and excitement, of big doings and coordinated plans coming to fruition, a bustling around the head table—sets this evening apart. Although I certainly am standing on home ground, I am also venturing into new territory. Tonight I will experience my first Passover Seder.

I locate Brian and Sarah, members of Bet Shira who had joined with me a couple of weeks previously to write haiku for this event. (The fourth poet in our group, Judith, is traveling tonight and cannot be at the Seder, so my husband, David, has volunteered to read her verse of our group poem.) We huddle in a corner of the room to plan our presentation. Because the group poem is circular in nature, with each verse linking to the one that comes before and the one that comes after, I want our reading to encircle and embrace all the people present. We decide that, when our turn comes in the evening's order of service, the four of us will move apart to stand in the four corners of the room. Then we will read our verses around the circle.

As we work out the plan, I stress the importance of speaking slowly, loudly, and clearly when reading haiku to a group of people who have never heard it before. Some people in the room might be using hearing aids. Others might need hearing aids and not have them. Still others will just not be listening all that carefully. Haiku is a very concentrated form of verse, and if you miss one word, you miss a good chunk of the experience. We want every word to be heard by every person in the room. I tell my fellow presenters that, in my experience, if an audience hears all the words, they feel happy and blessed. If they don't hear the words, they are uncomfortable and left out of the experience. It is as simple as that.

After assuring each other that we will be heard and deciding where each poet will stand, we are set for our presentation. We find our seats at the tables. Shortly after, Perry Spring, our leader through the fifteen-step order of service, welcomes everyone with "Happy Passover!" and an introduction of what is to come. We are off, on a multifaceted retelling of the Exodus story.

Perry gives a brief introduction to the foods on our table, and candles are lit with special blessings for Shabbat (it is Friday evening) and the holiday. We pour each other a first cup of wine, join with Perry in blessing the cup, then sip. Using water pitchers and basins provided at every table, we ritually wash our hands. I am powerfully reminded of the moment near the start of the celebration of the Eucharist when the priest ritually washes her hands in front of the whole congregation. As a lay Eucharistic minister, I have often had the role of pouring the water over our priest's outstretched fingers and offering the linen towel to dry her hands. On this night, for the first time, I am the one holding out my hands for the water, and I feel pleasure and wonder at this unexpected reversal of symbolic roles.

In his introduction, Perry has told us that the ancient rabbis urged their people not only to retell the Passover story, but also to embellish it. The more they did so, the more they would be blessed and praised. And the Bet Shira Congregation certainly takes that advice to heart!

In the course of the evening, one scene after another of the age-old story of slavery, oppression, hope, courage, redemption, and freedom is retold and held up for all to experience again. Children run through obstacles set up between the tables, to demonstrate passing through difficulties to get to freedom. I join with others who sweep through the room like a great wave, then gather together at one end and split apart to make a "narrow passage" for the children to pass through to safety. We sing songs together. A gray-haired rap artist tells the story in hip-hop rhythms, to the delight of the whole room. The pieces of matzah at each table are ritually broken, passed around, and eaten, with one piece hidden away for the children to hunt and discover at the end of the night. Four times we raise our wineglasses in blessing and drink sips of the sweet wine.

> Haiku is a very concentrated form of verse, and if you miss one word, you miss a good chunk of the experience.

As we retell the story of Passover, bless our cups of wine, break our matzah and pass it to one another around the table, in

Linking to other voices leaves room for serendipity, and serendipity opens a door for deeper sensations and feelings to come out and play.

the words and actions of all these ancient rites, I hear and feel the deep, deep history of the Eucharist, celebrated every Sunday in my church next door.

We are about two and a half hours into the evening when Perry leads us in *Dayeinu*. This ancient song expresses the gratitude for the acts of God that freed the Hebrew people from slavery in Egypt, brought them through the wilderness to the land of Israel, and formed the faith that binds them into one people. At each of God's acts, the people respond "*Dayeinu!*"—a way of saying, "For that alone, we would have been grateful!" or, "It would have been enough!"

If God had only created the world and not brought us out of Egypt, it would have been enough: *Dayeinu*!

If God had only brought us out of Egypt, but had not given us the Sabbath: *Dayeinu*!

If God had only given us the Sabbath, but had not given us the Torah: *Dayeinu*!

The *Dayeinu* song, which we had used as the inspiration for our haiku, is our cue. After the last "*Dayeinu*," Perry introduces me, and while the other three presenters move to opposite corners of the room, I give a short introduction to our process for writing the haiku poem they are about to hear. I also describe haiku as short and focused, saying that our presentation will be brief. My goal is to get the room into an alert, listening state, but the news that this part of the program will not last long also seems to brighten the crowd up a bit. One gentleman lifts his glass to me in a good-natured toast.

After my introduction, we read the poem around twice, starting and ending on the same haiku verse, so that the circular nature of the poem is revealed. The traditional *Dayeinu* song in Hebrew is quite long, evoking both gratitude and astonishment at the overwhelming abundance of God's acts. A modified and shortened version is commonly used at contemporary Seders, and that is the case on this night. But when we had met to write the haiku, we had included all the sections, so as not to leave out anything for inspiration. Following the steps of *lectio divina,* we had read again and again through all God's acts in the Passover story—the escape from Egypt, the defeat of the Egyptians, the splitting of the Sea of Reeds, the manna in the wilderness, the institution of the Sabbath, the gift of the Torah, and the arrival into the land of Israel—exclaiming at each part, "*Dayeinu!*" In the process, we had been filled by a strong sense of new birth: the birth of a people, the rebirth of all of us that night, and the possibility of new birth for anyone open to the call of freedom. The result was a group poem whose condensed language includes both the joy and the pain of new life.

> *ginkō:* a haiku walk, traditionally with two parts—people taking a walk in nature to compose haiku, then coming together to share and evaluate their poems

Here is the linked haiku poem we offered at the community Seder, with Brian's haiku as the starting and ending verse:

PASSOVER HAIKU
DAYEINU!

the river runs dry
only the chosen can cross   Brian
so we can be born

born of watermarks
slippery tears split aqua tide   Sarah
sea crowning dry land

under a wild sea
the earth's heart breaks open   Margaret
into birth

up and born
away from another world   Judith
shining and stained

the river runs dry
only the chosen can cross   Brian
so we can be born

The complete reading, twice over, takes only a few moments. Someone who is at the Seder later describes it to me as "a beautiful and potent addition to our ceremony." As our words encircle all the people in the room, I think how wonderful it is that a late-blooming Episcopalian like me might take part in such an ancient celebration, knowing that its stories are being retold that night in homes and synagogues all over the globe.

When the time finally comes for the festive meal, we are ready and the food abundant. No one had brought deviled eggs, and yet, I do not miss them. I eat my first bowl of matzah ball soup. Then—a seasoned hand at community meals—I fill my plate with small portions of every other dish on offer, and eat and eat.

It is nearing 10:00 p.m. when Perry says the last blessing over us, and I walk out into the spring night, tired, happy, and vowing that my first Seder will not be my last.

Practice: Door to Serendipity

Like many writers, I am a control freak when it comes to my own words. I hone and polish until the sentences line up "just so." This allows me the comforting—and perhaps somewhat delusional—sense of being in charge of what I am trying to say. It is a surprising relief to give up a bit of that control for the sake of linking my haiku with the poems of others. Linking to other voices leaves room for serendipity, and serendipity opens a door for deeper sensations and feelings to come out and play.

This Door to Serendipity practice describes a technique for creating a circular linked haiku poem in a group.

- Before writing linked haiku, your group will need a subject for shared inspiration. You might choose an inspirational poem, such as "Every Particle in the World Is a Mirror." Or a poetic text from the Bible, such as a favorite psalm or an excerpt from the Song of Solomon, might provide the inspiration you need. Whether you start with a poem or other text, choose one with poetic language—concrete images and words that evoke the senses—rather than the language of abstract ideas and theories.

  If your group comes together to write haiku for a particular event, such as a birthday or religious holiday, it helps to focus on an object or text that is closely associated with the event. For example, you might choose a collection of photographs for a birthday, a family menorah for Hanukkah, or the story of the Magi's visit for Epiphany.

  Another simple and traditional approach for a group to share haiku inspiration is to participate in a *ginkō,* or haiku walk. The group collects at a location, often a historic or scenic place. Everyone walks about jotting down notes of sensory impressions (smell, touch, sight, sound, taste, movement) as well as memories, thoughts, and feelings. After a period of time, group members join together again to write haiku, using their notes for material.

- Whatever you use for shared inspiration, allow plenty of time for everyone to experience it and jot down notes before starting to write haiku. If the group's focus is an object, allow time for members to describe it on paper as completely as possible, then go on to note any thoughts or feelings that arise. If it is a poem or other text, you might use the steps of *lectio divina* to help the group create individual lists of source materials. The idea is for each person in the group to start with plenty of notes—images, words, personal thoughts, and feelings—all pointing back to the group's shared inspiration.

- Sitting with your group in a circle, invite group members to look over their notes and pick out one word that rises up to them with special energy—a word they would like to use in a haiku. Ask them to write that word at the top of a clean page of paper, then write it again at the *bottom* of the page.

- Instruct them to tear the word off the bottom of the page and pass it to the person on their right. Now each person will have two words—the one they wrote, and the one they received.

  Note: If people happen to receive the same word that they passed (it happens!), they should pass it back and ask the person to pass them another word. Do not go on to the next step until each person in the group has two different words: one passed and one received.

- Ask group members to write a haiku that includes both the word they passed and the word they received. Let them know that it is okay to use a form of either word.

For example, if you passed or received the word *sun*, it would be okay to use *sunny* in your haiku.

- After everyone has written a haiku, start anywhere in the circle and read the poems aloud, in order, around the ring. Remind everyone to read the haiku slowly and clearly, and to leave a little time between haiku. Listen for the words that flow around the circle, linking one haiku verse to the next.

  Note: Your group poem can start and end at any point, and can be read clockwise or counterclockwise. Try reading the poem one way around, and then the other way around. Does a different feeling rise out of the changed direction?

- Congratulations on your group poem! To make a record of your collaboration, have those in the circle write a clean copy of their haiku and sign it. Number the verses so that it will be easy to keep them in sequence. Then ask for a volunteer to put the individual haiku together for distribution to everyone.

- It can be enlightening to exchange feedback on the group process. How did using a word that you didn't choose yourself affect your writing? How was it limiting, and how was it freeing? Is there one unifying theme that rose out of your collective creative effort? How do you understand the process as the Creative Spirit at work among you?

The serendipity that happens in the group poem comes from the passed word. When you include a word in your creation that you did not choose yourself, a door opens to a place you may never get to without serendipity's help.

How do you open that door to serendipity in your individual poems? By giving up some control. Here's a way to practice this on your own:

- In the coming week, choose a text, an object, or a place to use as inspiration, then fill a page of paper with sensory notes, memories, and feelings that arise from it. Use the steps of *lectio divina* or any other method that works for you to produce your source material.

- When you have a full page, use scissors to cut the words apart. Discard all the articles and little words, such as *the*, *is*, and *to*. Keep sensory words and concrete nouns, such as *sky*, regardless of how short they are. Put all your words in a small container, such as a bowl, bag, or box.

- Copy a favorite poem or sacred text, then do the same with it. Cut the words apart, discarding articles and keeping sensory words and concrete nouns. Put them in a separate container. Every day for a week, draw one word from each container and write a haiku containing those two words.

- At the end of the week, look over your haiku. Where did serendipity take you that you might never have gone on your own?

CHAPTER SEVEN

Haiku with Pictures or Prose

He who binds to himself a joy
Does the winged life destroy;
But he who kisses the joy as it flies
Lives in Eternity's sunrise.
                    —*William Blake (1757–1827)*

I like to imagine a meeting between William Blake and the great masters of Japanese haiku. It seems to me they would have plenty to talk about. I can picture the poet Blake, a skilled engraver and illustrator who ran a print shop for most of his life, exchanging business tips with the renowned woman haiku poet Chiyo-ni, who operated her family's scroll-making business after the deaths of her parents and brother. At a dinner party of my imagination, Chiyo-ni and Blake engage in lively discussions with the four men most often named as masters of classical Japanese haiku—Matsuo Bashō, Yosa Buson, Kobayashi Issa, and Masaoka Shiki—on topics such as the roles of imagination and experience in poetry, the way transience and eternity entwine in each passing moment, or what it means to defy convention in art and life.

Most of all, I imagine Blake finding it a great relief to talk to other poets who illustrate their poems with their own paintings, and who think it a perfectly natural thing to do. Blake's strange and visionary paintings would have made him an odd duck in any time or place. However, when he put them together with his poems and published those poem-paintings in books, he became a truly rare bird in the annals of Western art, where poets generally stick to words and painters, to visual images. In contrast, the "three perfections"—calligraphy, painting, and poetry—are traditionally viewed in East Asia as one unified art. Over ages, paintings from that region have commonly contained brief lines of poetry rendered in calligraphy as part of their overall design.

Words and visual images together convey layers of meaning, expressing more than what is possible to say in either words or pictures alone.

Bashō, the first great haiku master, wrote his travel journals and poetry with *sumi* ink and brush, and he used the same familiar writing tools to add visual images to his writings. Although Bashō was carrying on a long cultural tradition of combining painting with poetry, his modest little brush-and-ink sketches stand apart from the elegance of classical Chinese and Japanese painting in the same way that his haiku stand apart from the elevated style of imperial court poetry. Bashō used simple and direct language in his poetry, and he took the same approach in his painting, allowing a few rough brushstrokes to evoke a morning glory vine, a banana tree, or a hut by the side of the road.

This basic approach for combining visual elements with haiku became increasingly popular among poets. A few of the great haiku poets, such as Buson and Chiyo-ni, were also recognized as master painters, but for most others, these small, rough paintings became more about the practice of *seeing* than about developing technical skill as a painter. Just as the haiku poet expresses the heart of a moment in a few plain words, the painter tries to convey something of the essence of what is seen in a few simple brushstrokes. In this way, painting opens up another pathway for entering into the moment at hand, expanding awareness and relationship with the energies that enliven our world. Words and visual images together convey layers of meaning, expressing more than what is possible to say in either words or pictures alone.

Sumi-e and the Four Treasures

Sumi-e, which literally means "black ink painting," grew out of a style of painting that came to Japan from China around the fourteenth century CE. The Japanese embraced the approach, which uses black *sumi* ink in gradations of shades and concentrations, and adapted it to their own cultural style. *Sumi-e* requires four basic tools, called the "Four Treasures":

- an *ink stone,* carved with a shallow depression and used to prepare and hold the ink for the work at hand.
- an *ink stick,* made of compressed soot bound with resin. Many ink sticks are beautifully carved with bas-relief calligraphy and dragons or natural elements.
- a *brush,* usually animal hair in bamboo. The brush hairs taper to a fine point so that the painter can move from the finest to the widest line in a single stroke.
- *paper,* often rice paper because of its superior properties in absorbing the ink. *Sumi-e* is also sometimes painted on silk.

To begin, the painter sprinkles a small amount of water on the ink stone, then holding the ink stick upright, rubs it in a smooth circular motion against the wet stone, releasing soot into the water to make ink. The painter makes just enough ink for the work at hand.

Inexpensive *sumi-e* beginner's kits containing ink stone, ink stick, and one or two brushes are available in art stores and online. The tools fit comfortably in a small travel box, making *sumi-e* a type of art that you can easily take on the road with you.

The Art of *Haiga*

From the work of haiku poet-painters, a type of artwork called *haiga* developed, in which a haiku written in calligraphy appears as part of a spare, sketchlike ink painting. The painted image in a *haiga* is not necessarily a direct illustration of the haiku. The two might simply be related in some way, and showing them together is an attempt to bring the relationship to life.

day begins
the skylights yellow
with tree pollen

mdm

Today, *haiga* come in all styles and colors, including photographs, collage, and even animation. The haiku might appear in a type-face that the artist chose for the way it goes with the visual image. Although you will find modern *haiga* in most any medium that can put images and text together (check out the broad range of *haiga* posted on websites), the tradition of combining *sumi* ink sketches with haiku rendered in calligraphy continues to provide fertile ground for new artwork.

The simple, homely style of traditional *haiga* relates to *wabi-sabi,* a way of seeing beauty and life that reaches so deeply into Japanese history and culture, it might be described as a world-view rather than a set of artistic principles. Impossible to translate directly, *wabi-sabi* involves appreciation for the spiritual gifts of poverty and loneliness, along with the beauty of things that have aged naturally over time.

The inner beauty of *wabi-sabi* is found in the essentials of a simple and sometimes lonely life, rather than in the hectic materialism of the modern world. The outer beauty of *wabi-sabi* is found in a rustic earthenware pot, chipped and stained with use, rather than in the elegant perfection of an intricately glazed porcelain vase. My mother's memories of summer visits to her grandparent's small Depression-era farm are awash in *wabi-sabi,* and so are certain of my own recollections, such as a memory of sitting by myself on a rock next to the creek in Tawawa Park in my Ohio hometown, eating a peanut butter sandwich, watching crawdads swim, and waiting for my frayed old sneakers to dry in the sun.

haiga: a combination of haiku (often in calligraphy) with a visual image

If brevity is one of haiku's great strengths, it is also one of the form's limitations. In three brief lines, I cannot convey the complexity of the memories from the banks of my childhood creek, clear and evocative as they may be in my own consciousness. A picture would help—a photograph of a creek lined with trees and strewn with big rocks, perhaps, or even a sketch of a crawdad in water. Then I could choose other images for my haiku that would expand and deepen the feelings evoked by the picture.

wabi-sabi: appreciation for the spiritual gifts of poverty and loneliness, along with the beauty of things that have aged naturally over time

Here the haiku form's brevity turns back into its strength, because the shortness of a haiku helps it fit easily in the context of a painting, photograph, or other type of picture. The haiku's few words can be absorbed in a glance along with the visual image, so that each enriches the whole without distracting from the other.

The Art of *Haibun*

Similarly, the pithiness of a haiku makes it a fine companion to prose writing. Scattered throughout a travel journal or a diary, a series of haiku can provide a range of quick impressions in mood and color, without breaking the flow of the narrative the way longer poems do. This form of writing that mixes haiku and prose is called *haibun*. A *haibun* may contain just a few lines of prose juxtaposed with one haiku, or it may continue for many pages of prose interwoven with haiku.

The quintessential example of haiku and prose working together is also one of the best-known works of its kind, Bashō's *Oku no Hosomichi,* or *Narrow Road to the Interior.* Based on a travel diary that the poet kept on one of his long walking journeys, this small book recounts the journey's events in quiet, unsentimental language that draws the reader in without rendering judgment

haibun: a mixture of haiku and prose

on what is happening. Interspersed among the prose passages are haiku, some of which Bashō wrote on the road to be shared at *renga* parties and social engagements that took place during his journey. *Oku no Hosomichi* is revered as a national classic in Japan, and it is also widely recognized as one of the great works of world literature.

Haibun vary widely in style, depending on the approach and aim of the individual writer. Like haiku, *haibun* work best with a subject matter of everyday things presented just the way they are, without much interpretation from the writer. Just as a visual image and a haiku work together in *haiga* to make a single unified picture, prose and poetry work together in *haibun* to bring a scene or series of moments to life. Ideally, the haiku in a *haibun* do not merely restate the events of the prose, but complement the prose in some way, allowing the reader to discover and enjoy the relationship between the two.

I wrote the following *haibun* after a trip to help my parents move into an assisted living apartment in their retirement community. It was the season of Lent when I wrote the first draft, and I included short passages of Lenten scripture readings that expressed some of the feeling behind the conversations and events surrounding the move. A diary I had kept on the road helped me remember impressions and conversations that had resonance at the time, and I interspersed prose, scripture, and haiku to make a single short piece.

Haibun work best with a subject matter of everyday things presented just the way they are, without much interpretation from the writer.

> Driving to my brother's house on a clear winter day. Mt. Rainier floats on the horizon, a great silent pink and white dome with fissures of blue.
>
> Left home with a sense of having forgotten something. All along the drive trying to think what it was. Nothing comes to me.
>
> Stayed in the car during the ferry ride across Puget Sound, then followed the long line of cars from the ferry out to Seattle's city streets. After three blocks, traffic stopped dead by a long, slow freight train. Some drivers lose patience and make U-turns, but I know only one way.

> ah, sun on my arm ...
> with the air inversion
> comes Dad's asthma

Finally the end of the train—not a caboose this time, but an engine facing backward.

It is growing dark. From the I-90 bridge, fir trees on the island stand black against the deepening sky. An uneventful trip, and yet my neck is stiff before the turn onto my brother's street. Tomorrow I will spend the day with my parents, helping them winnow down their possessions and make decisions about what to take into assisted living.

I am poured out like water, and all my bones are out of joint; my heart is like wax; it is melted within my breast ...

—PSALM 22:14

The next afternoon, Mom and I take a break while Dad goes out for more boxes. She tells me that in the days and weeks that followed her stroke, at times lying in her bed at the health center, she would feel alone and frightened. She says that when she felt in greatest need, she would pray for someone to come, and that someone always came. From this, she believes that God is taking care of her.

For surely I know the plans I have for you ... plans for your welfare and not harm, to give you a future with hope.... When you search for me, you will find me; if you seek me with all your heart.

—JEREMIAH 29:11, 13

Immediately after the stroke, my mother had nightmares of being held captive in the basement of a ruined mansion, with broken debris from the building all around her. She tells me that in one dream, she was huddled in the corner of that basement, alone and afraid. In the dream, she prayed for help, and help came.

splintered door jamb
mother's power wheelchair
fitting through

My father returns from the store with a carload of empty boxes. We rejoice in fresh resources, then start to work on the kitchen cabinets. Almost everything will end up at the thrift shop, and these boxes are just the right size.

> Good Friday …
> in my dream I am blind, dreaming
> of light

William Blake and Japanese haiku masters had a lot in common. They wrote great poems that still touch our feelings. They joined their verse with other art forms, creating composite works that still delight. Above all, they stayed true to their visions, with the courage to experiment in bringing those visions to life. A haiku expresses the heart of a moment in a few brief lines. When that heart calls out for flesh, bones, hands, and face, then haiku is ready to work in the company of any medium your imagination requires to make your vision whole.

> Haiku is ready to work in the company of any medium your imagination requires to make your vision whole.

Practice: Keeping It Light

Are you ready to put haiku together with a visual image? If you are comfortable working with images, your answer might be, "Sure, lead me to it!" If not, you may be thinking, "I can't do art, so this practice is not for me"—in which case, I understand and empathize. My hand-eye coordination must have been slow to develop as a child because everything I made in art class at school was truly awful. As a result, I grew up convinced that my talents lay elsewhere. It has taken many years of doodling around in one medium or another, intermixed with deep-set resistance, for me to admit, first, that I want to make things, and second, that wanting to do it is the whole ball of wax. Next to desire, talent does not really matter at all.

And yet, all those old voices saying that I am no good at art are still in my head, ready to wake up and start yapping if I so much as sidle into a professional art supply store and begin to browse through the tubes of paint. So when I set out to do some art, it helps me to start by keeping it light, the better not to wake those bad guys up. Fortunately, keeping it light works just fine when combining haiku with visual images.

However you feel about making art, for the next few moments, I ask you to put all thought of what you can and cannot do aside, and just follow these steps. You will need a few pieces of blank white paper and a black ink pen, black crayon, or a kid's watercolor paint set that includes the color black.

- On the upper left quadrant of a sheet of paper, draw a circle in black. It does not have to be a perfect circle.

- Starting in the lower left quadrant of the page, draw a diagonal line from the left edge of the sheet up and across to the right edge, ending a little above the middle of the page. It does not have to be a straight line.

- In the paper's upper right quadrant, closer to the top of the quadrant than to the bottom, write the name of the current season and the word *moon*. For example, "spring moon" or "autumn moon."
- Look outside. Look as far into the distance as possible, then gradually bring your gaze close at hand.
- On a separate piece of paper, jot down an image or two from what you just saw. Without too much editing, turn one of those images into the second and third lines of a haiku.
- Write those two lines beneath the moon line on the first piece of paper.

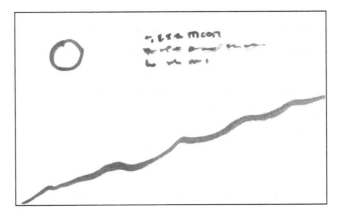

- Congratulations! You have created a *haiga* for the moon, one of the classic haiku themes. Tape that beauty up on a wall.

Now that you have made your first *haiga*, you are set to explore this art form wherever the Spirit leads. Here is one idea for the coming week. If this sounds like fun, try it out. If it sparks another idea you like better, try that instead. Just remember to keep it light!

- Look ahead on your calendar to an upcoming birthday for an adult friend or family member. Find an old photograph of that person—a baby or childhood picture might work well, or for an older person, a picture from youth.

- Keep that picture in your mind as you go about your daily life, and look for images in the world that make you think of the person or the photograph. Take notes and write some haiku. (Try writing at least one haiku that does not name the person directly, but that contains only images from your life today that you connect to the photograph or person.) After you have a number of haiku to choose from, pick one to use as a message on a card.

- Acquire a scan or color copy of the photograph, and combine that image with your haiku to make the card. You can use graphics software to put the two together, or scissors and paste also work just fine. You can write your haiku in your own handwriting, or you can use a word processing program and choose a font you like. Play with the words and the image until you like the way they look together.

- Congratulations on your *haiga*! This will be a special card that the recipient will want to keep.

To integrate haiku, prose, and pictures into your daily spiritual practice, all you need is a small notebook and a willing spirit. Here is a way to carry your practice out into the world and make it a part of your life.

- Take your notebook with you wherever you go. When a moment comes that touches your innermost heart, pause, look, and listen. In the spirit of haiku, do not worry about what the moment *means*, but simply try to see what it *is*.

- What do you see? Jot down an image in words, or make a quick sketch. Let go of all your preconceived notions and do your best to reflect back what you see truly, without interpretation. When you sincerely try to see into the heart of another object or being, your own heart becomes vulnerable and opens in response.

- What is happening in the outer world right now? The answer to that question might take a sentence or two.

- What is happening in your inner world right now? The answer to that question might also take a sentence or two.

- At the end of the week, set aside some time to go through your jottings. You might think of this as Sabbath time, a time of gathering together and integrating the week past. Choose from among your images and musings, and create one piece that includes prose, haiku, and a sketch or two. This single unified piece shows where your spirit went in the past week, what it encountered, and how it grew.

- Begin anew in the coming week, taking your small notebook and your willing spirit with you wherever you go.

- At the end of the month or year, go back and look at all you have created from this exercise. You may discover something about how God's spirit meets up with your spirit to work together in everyday life.

CHAPTER EIGHT

The Haiku Life

there is no ending
only
the change of seasons
—Doris Horton Thurston

A greeting is an opening between one and another. When my neighbor and I meet on the lane, "Hello" opens the way for conversation. Even if no more words are said at the moment, the door is ajar. The habit of exchanging hellos makes it that much easier to step across the threshold into deeper conversation.

A haiku is an expression of openness to God's creation, just as it is. Like a "Hello," the brevity of haiku allows for no more than a moment of recognition, with time for a brief reply. The best topics for this sort of casual meeting are small things, close at hand—the same small things that, over time, come together to make a day, a season, a year, a life.

> Everything has a heart. It bears on us to be sensitive to the beating of little hearts and big hearts in places we don't necessarily expect them to be. Everything wants to be worthy, loved, accepted into the whole. It is one of the haiku poet's duties to pay attention to small things.
>
> —KARMA TENZING WANGCHUK

In paying attention to small things, the haiku poet honors the sacredness of everyday life. Making a habit of writing haiku is a way to practice awareness of the moment at hand. When you write haiku regularly, you create patterns in your life for expressing wonder and joy at creation. Those patterns turn out to be maps, showing the way to discovery of the Spirit that lives in each of us.

> A haiku is an expression of openness to God's creation, just as it is.

Following are a few suggestions for integrating the spiritual practice of haiku into your days and beginning to live the haiku life.

Get in the Haiku Habit

Most of my habits, bad and good, were formed without my knowing quite how they came to be. But it is possible for me to make a new habit on purpose, if I choose to do it and then stick with the plan.

Does it sound crazy to choose to write a haiku a day? If you require perfection from every haiku you write, then yes—it is crazy. But if all you ask of yourself is one moment's attention with a heartfelt response, then writing a haiku a day is perfectly doable. Many serious haiku writers will write thousands, sometimes tens of thousands, of haiku during their lifetimes. Those I have talked with readily admit that most of what they produce is not great art. One poet with many publications told me that if he wrote a single haiku out of a hundred that held up over time, he felt he was doing pretty well.

> In paying attention to small things, the haiku poet honors the sacredness of everyday life.

Here is a challenge for you: *for one hundred days, write a haiku a day with little or no editing.* Just jot down the images and be finished. At the end of the hundred days, go back to read through them all. I bet you will find a few gold nuggets amid the pebbles. You will also find a record of events and feelings to reconnect you to a whole season of your life.

One way to get started in your haiku-a-day habit is to integrate the practice with a habit you already have, such as taking a walk, cooking a meal, or reading a daily devotional. Use your existing habit as an inspiration and a springboard for your daily haiku. After some practice, writing the haiku will turn into a habit on its own.

Another way to get started is to give yourself a topic, a piece of grit to start your daily pearl. For example, what is the next holiday with special meaning for you in the calendar? Write a haiku a day around themes from that holiday, right up to the day itself. Reading over your haiku might be part of your holiday celebration. There is nothing wrong with repeating the same topic day after day. After a week or so, you might be surprised at all you have to say

Here is a challenge for you: *for one hundred days, write a haiku a day with little or no editing.*

and find yourself unwilling to give up your haiku writing when the holiday arrives. Look ahead to the next holiday and start again.

You can also mine this book's practices for topics ideas. For example, you might go back to your list of sacred places, developed from the practice at the end of chapter 4. Choose one place to start with and write a haiku about that place every day, sticking with the same place as your theme for at least a week. Or go back to the practice at the end of chapter 2 on writing haiku as prayer. At the end of each day, write a haiku as a prayer of praise for one moment or one image from this day that stayed with you all the way to bedtime. If your spiritual practice includes reading a daily devotional with a passage from scripture, try writing a haiku inspired by the day's passage, using the process of *lectio divina* outlined in chapter 5.

The simplest and least contrived topic for a daily haiku is the day itself. Look outside—what's happening out there? Sun or clouds? Flowers in the garden or snow on the ground? Open up to the moment at hand, and let that moment's voice provide your topic. Being alive and aware in the moment is the best spiritual exercise I know. A haiku can provide the motivation for you to stretch and grow in awe of all creation.

> Being alive and aware in the moment is the best spiritual exercise I know.

Self-assigned topics make good training wheels and fun, enlightening exercises. However, once you are in the haiku habit, you will probably not need them. Instead, each day, the subject of your haiku will come to you.

Find a Good Book to Read

For anyone who wants to delve deeper into haiku, my first advice is to get yourself to your local library or bookstore and find a good translation of Bashō's *Oku no Hosomichi,* the journal of his travels in Japan's north country. Of the translations I have read, my favorite is Sam Hamill's *Narrow Road to the Interior* for its engaging prose style and graceful rendering of Bashō's haiku, and for Stephen Addiss's beautiful and evocative illustrations. Another fine translation is Hiroaki Sato's *Bashō's Narrow Road: Spring and Autumn Passages*. I especially appreciate Sato's bountiful notes, which illuminate the many historical and literary references in Bashō's masterpiece. Sato's book includes an added bonus: it is illustrated with charming *sumi-e* paintings made for Bashō's work by the master painter and haiku poet Yosa Buson.

Every time I read Bashō's small travel journal from a distant time and place, I find myself looking into my own world with a smile and an open heart, itching to take to the road and write haiku.

Another excellent resource is R. H. Blyth, whose brief quotations from his four-volume work *Haiku* are scattered throughout this book. Blyth lived in Japan during the middle part of the twentieth century and wrote extensively about haiku and Zen Buddhism, his twin passions. Although he is criticized for finding a closer relationship between the two than may actually exist, Blyth's deep love of haiku pours out from every page of his work, and his translations of classic haiku speak to the heart.

If you are interested in the art and craft of writing haiku, excellent contemporary guides are available to sharpen your skills. I especially recommend *The Haiku Handbook: How to Write, Share, and Teach Haiku,* by William J. Higginson with Penny Harter, and Lee Gurga's *Haiku: A Poet's Guide.* These accessible texts offer a solid grounding in the form, practical suggestions for writing and editing your haiku, and a flood of great examples.

Above all, read haiku from many sources. Read the old masters and the young rebels. I found inspiration from the classics in *The Essential Haiku: Versions of Bashō, Buson, and Issa*, edited by Robert Hass, and from *Chiyo-ni: Woman Haiku Master*, by Patricia Donegan and Yoshie Ishibashi. Cor van den Heuvel's *The Haiku Anthology: Haiku and Senryū in English* contains an outstanding selection of contemporary English-language haiku. Patricia Donegan's *Haiku Mind: 108 Poems to Cultivate Awareness and Open Your Heart* presents both classic and contemporary haiku with brief meditations by the author and information about the poets' lives.

An astonishing number of new haiku are being written and published every year, and an even more astonishing number of words have been written and published about the form over many years. Although my suggestions just scratch the surface of what's available, this listing is a way for me to share with you a few of my own favorites. You will find more resources in the Haiku Resources section at the end of this book, and more still in bookstores, libraries, and on the Web.

Make Haiku Friends

Witnessing my world by writing a haiku makes me feel good. Sharing my haiku with a sympathetic listener is an extension of that good feeling, for myself and—I hope—for the listener, too. When I show my haiku to other haiku poets, who share their work with me in turn, a circle comes round and we inspire each other. Today people all around the globe are writing haiku. A haiku poet who would like to exchange haiku with you and talk about the haiku life might live just down the street. All you need to do is find each other.

The Haiku Society of America (HSA) provides a great resource for making connections with other haiku poets. Their website, www.hsa-haiku.org, contains contact information for regional chapters along with a wealth of material about haiku contests, publications, society meetings, and news from the world of haiku. The HSA site also includes links to haiku discussion groups and forums, webzines, instructional material, and the sites of individual haiku poets.

Haiku webzines and forums are a good source of ideas for topics and exercises, as well as places to make haiku friends. A forum might sponsor a monthly *kukai,* a relaxed kind of poetry contest, in which the contestants choose the winners among themselves. Poets submit haiku on an assigned topic, and the submissions are posted anonymously. Those who submit poems have the opportunity to vote by giving points to the haiku they like best among all the submissions. Results are tallied and distributed at the end of the month. A new topic is then posted and the process starts again.

My own website, In the Courtyard (www.inthecourtyard.com), has a page called *Lectio*+Haiku, where you can respond to a passage from a sacred text of one of the world's faith traditions with a haiku. Each month I post a new passage, and readers send in original haiku that we post next to the passage. The result is a poetic exchange on themes from sacred writings of the world.

> Listening to the haiku of others and sharing your own on a common spiritual theme opens multiple pathways for its meaning to enter your heart.

Your public library may also be a resource for finding nearby haiku poets. The librarian may know of an existing haiku group, or the library might maintain a bulletin board where you could post a few of your haiku along with a query about sharing haiku with another person.

You might consider forming a haiku group at your church or place of worship. Set up a schedule of regular meetings, just as any other continuing spiritual growth group would do. Within the group, you can develop assignments for mutual haiku inspiration, such as themes for an upcoming religious holiday, or scripture texts for upcoming services. Then take the current

> Unless I offer this moment the awareness and attention that are mine to give, how can I know its heart?

assignment out into daily life and write haiku on that theme, bringing your haiku to share at the next meeting. Listening to the haiku of others and sharing your own on a common spiritual theme opens multiple pathways for its meaning to enter your heart. For more ideas on writing haiku together as a group and sharing what you write with your larger faith community, see chapter 6, "Haiku in Community."

One of the best ways to find other haiku poets is simply to write haiku and not keep it a secret. Append your daily haiku to your e-mail. Make cards with your haiku and use them for birthdays or other occasions. One day, you are sure to receive a haiku in return.

Go Outside and Greet the World

It is time for me to stop writing, and for you to stop reading, and for each of us to go outside and greet the world.

> daybreak
> the slug beat me
> to the strawberry
> —M.D.M.

Because, though writing and reading are certainly elements of the haiku life, they are not the point of it. No haiku I ever write will have as much life in it as the next breath I take.

> For me, haiku is more than a form of written expression; it's a practice that helps me to wake up and live more abundantly.
>
> —CHRISTOPHER HEROLD

A haiku expresses the heart of a moment in a few brief lines. Unless I offer this moment the awareness and attention that are mine to give, how can I know its heart?

June morning
a breeze in the meadow
loosens strings

      June morning
      from east and west
      robins *cheeriup*

            June morning
            the crick in my neck
            is gone

                  —M.D.M.

So I leave you with advice from the master on how to live the haiku life—a life with room enough to hold both truth and joy.

> Make the universe your companion, always bearing in mind the true nature of things—mountains and rivers, trees and grasses, and humanity—and enjoy the falling blossoms and the scattering leaves.
>
> —BASHŌ

I hope you are inspired to go out and greet the world. If so, I suggest you take along pencil and paper, because the world will reply in kind, and you will surely want to jot down a few notes.

ACKNOWLEDGMENTS

From my heart, deep bows of gratitude:
To my haiku teachers, starting with Carol Light, who helped me find the poet lurking within this prosaic self. At the Port Townsend Haiku Club, I met a dedicated group of experienced haiku writers who welcomed me in, shared their work and creative process, and helped me connect to the larger haiku community. I am especially grateful to Karma Tenzing Wangchuk for enlightening conversation and e-mail that broadened and deepened my understanding of the haiku form, and to Christopher Herold, for wise and gentle critiques of my haiku, generous sharing from his library of haiku books, and conversation about how haiku has affected his own spiritual life. I hope that every haiku student may find such a teacher and friend. Christopher read an early draft of this book and made suggestions that saved me from a number of fumbles and errors. Those that remain are mine alone.

To the many scholars and teachers of haiku whose work informed and inspired my own, with special thanks for insights on the haiku form to Lee Gurga, William Higginson, Penny Harter, and R. H. Blyth. For information on the history and development of haiku and related forms, as well as how haiku are written today, I am also particularly indebted to the writings of Stephen Addiss, Faubion Blowers, Patricia Donegan, Jeanne Emrich, Sam Hamill, Robert Hass, Jim Kacian, Tom Lowenstein, A. C. Missias, Jane Reichhold, Hiroaki Sato, Haruo Shirane, George Swede, and Michael Dylan Welch.

The practices that appear at the end of chapters in this book contain approaches and ideas that percolated out of many exercises and group writing activities I encountered during the writing life. I am grateful to all the creative people who think up interesting things for other creative people to do, with a particular awareness of my debts to Sheila Bender, Nancy Chickerneo, William Higginson, Carol Light, and Timothy Russell.

To the many fine poets who gave me permission to use their work, and whose wonderful poems bring this book to life, I remain forever grateful. Special thanks to Sheikh Jamal Rahman and Sally Jo Gilbert de Vargas at the Interfaith Community Church in Seattle, Washington, and to Stephanie Reith, Brian Rohr, and Perry Spring of the Port Townsend Bet Shira Congregation, for help in putting together the workshops and community events that appear as examples in this book.

To all those who responded to my survey on sacred places, thank you for sharing your sacred places, and most especially for sharing what makes them sacred to you.

To my faith community at St. Paul's, with special thanks to the Rev. Elizabeth A. Bloch, Tom Christopher, and the Women's Spiritual Growth Group, who will drop everything to write haiku with me: Donna Cheshier, Katie Fleming, Val Johnstone, Kate Spear, and Sue Taylor.

To my writers group, who showed up for extra meetings in the heat of the writing and gave early drafts of these chapters the great gifts of their attention and sharp critique: Judith Collins Glass, Carolyn Latteier, and David Schroeder.

To SkyLight Paths for believing in this book, with special thanks to my editor Marcia Broucek—such a joy to work with, ever calm and supporting, with skillful aim to make the book all that it is trying to be. Special thanks also to Emily Wichland, Lauren Hill, Kristi Menter, and Jenny Buono for their talent and dedication in putting the pieces together to make a beautiful book.

To my family for their love and support, and most especially for David, whose love means everything to me.

HAIKU RESOURCES

Haiku is widely read and written in the world today, and thousands of websites, journals, and organizations are devoted to nurturing and publishing new haiku. This listing presents some of the print and online resources that I and my haiku friends have found interesting and useful. Many of the websites listed below include links pages that will connect you to additional resources.

Organizations and Associations

BRITISH HAIKU SOCIETY

38 Wayside Ave., Hornchurch, Essex RM12 4LL, UK
www.haikusoc.ndo.co.uk

Sponsors events such as discussion groups, workshops, and haiku walks, and holds an annual conference. Publishes *Blithe Spirit*, a journal of haiku by society members, as well as essays, book reviews, and contests.

HAIKU CANADA

www.haikucanada.org

Sponsors weekend events and an annual conference; publishes a newsletter with haiku, essays, reviews, and information about upcoming contests and events.

THE HAIKU FOUNDATION

P.O. Box 2461, Winchester, VA 22604-1661
http://thehaikufoundation.org

A nonprofit, volunteer organization whose aim is to preserve and archive the accomplishments of the first century of haiku in English, and to provide resources for its expansion in the next.

THE HAIKU SOCIETY OF AMERICA

P.O. Box 31, Nassau, NY 12123

www.hsa-haiku.org

Sponsors open lectures, workshops, readings, and contests; publishes *Frogpond* (see next page). Website includes information about upcoming events and contests as well as links to regional organizations.

WORLD HAIKU ASSOCIATION

www.worldhaiku.net

A worldwide, multilingual organization to recognize and encourage international standards for excellence in haiku. Sponsors events around the world and an annual international *haiga* contest.

Print and Online Journals

ACORN: A JOURNAL OF CONTEMPORARY HAIKU

http://home.earthlink.net/~missias/Acorn.html

Biannual print journal, published by redfox press.

BEAR CREEK HAIKU

P.O. Box 3787, Boulder, CO 80503

Print magazine, published six or seven times a year. Haiku and other short forms of verse.

BOTTLE ROCKETS

P.O. Box 189, Windsor, CT 06095

www.bottlerocketspress.com

Biannual print magazine. Haiku, *haibun*, and other haiku-like forms of short verse.

CONTEMPORARY HAIBUN ONLINE: A QUARTERLY JOURNAL OF CONTEMPORARY ENGLISH LANGUAGE HAIBUN

http://contemporaryhaibunonline.com

The quarterly online journal is associated with the annual print anthology *contemporary haibun,* published by Red Moon Press.

FROGPOND: THE JOURNAL OF THE HAIKU SOCIETY OF AMERICA

Print magazine, published three times a year. Contemporary English-language haiku and *senryū,* linked forms including sequences, *renku, renga,* and *haibun,* essays and articles on these forms, and book reviews. For more information, see the website of the Haiku Society of America (see previous page).

HAIGAONLINE

www.haigaonline.com

Biannual online journal of contemporary and traditional *haiga.*

THE HERON'S NEST

www.theheronsnest.com

Quarterly online haiku journal that also publishes an annual print edition.

LYNX: A JOURNAL FOR LINKING POETS

P.O. Box 767, Gualala, CA 95445
www.ahapoetry.com/ahalynx/241hmpg.html

Online journal published three times a year, including *renga* and other linked verse forms, essays, book reviews, and *haiga.*

MAYFLY

Brooks Books, 3720 N. Woodridge Dr., Decatur, IL 62526
www.brooksbookshaiku.com/mayfly.html

A biannual print journal of haiku, published by Brooks Books.

MODERN HAIKU: AN INDEPENDENT JOURNAL OF HAIKU AND HAIKU STUDIES

P.O. Box 33077, Santa Fe, NM 87594-9998

www.modernhaiku.org

Print journal published three times a year. Haiku and *senryū,* essays, book reviews.

ROADRUNNER

www.roadrunnerjournal.net

Quarterly online journal of haiku and related forms.

SIMPLY HAIKU: A QUARTERLY JOURNAL OF JAPANESE SHORT FORM POETRY

www.simplyhaiku.com

Online journal publishing short-form poetry, *haiga, haibun,* essays, interviews, and reviews.

SKETCHBOOK: A JOURNAL FOR EASTERN & WESTERN SHORT FORMS

www.poetrywriting.org

Bimonthly international online journal featuring poems, art, essays, contests, and more.

WISTERIA: A JOURNAL OF HAIKU, SENRYŪ, AND TANKA

P.O. Box 150932, Lufkin, TX 75915

http://wistaria.blogspot.com

Quarterly print journal.

Once-a-Day Haiku and *Haiga*

DAILYHAIGA: AN EDITED JOURNAL OF CONTEMPORARY AND TRADITIONAL *HAIGA*

www.dailyhaiga.org

New English-language *haiga* presented each day.

DAILYHAIKU

www.dailyhaiku.org

Also publishes an annual print collection.

ISSA HAIKU-A-DAY

http://cat.xula.edu/issa

Each day, a randomly chosen haiku from the Kobayashi Issa archive.

TINYWORDS

http://tinywords.com

Fresh haiku, delivered daily to your e-mail address.

Other Interesting Sites

AHA POETRY

www.ahapoetry.com

Maintained by haiku writer, teacher, and author Jane Reichhold, including tips, events, contests, and more.

BROOKS BOOKS HAIKU

www.brooksbookshaiku.com

Offers reviews, online collections of haiku and visual art, books, and other haiku-related publications in a variety of media.

"CONTEMPORARY HAIKU: ORIGINS AND NEW DIRECTIONS"

http://webdelsol.com/Perihelion/acmarticle.htm

An excellent essay by A. C. Missias.

LINKS TO HAIKU SITES

www.hawkscry.com/haiku/Haiklink.html

Maintained by Mark Alan Osterhaus.

MILLIKIN UNIVERSITY HAIKU

http://old.millikin.edu/haiku

Information on courses, conferences, and competitions, as well as student research on haiku and haiku poets.

SHIKI MONTHLY KUKAI

www.haikuworld.org/kukai

A peer-reviewed monthly haiku contest.

TEREBESS ASIA ONLINE'S "MODERN AMERICAN HAIKU POETS"

www.terebess.hu/english/usa/haiku.html

Biographies and sample haiku of many American poets.

NOTES

Poems not listed here are previously unpublished. Please see the Credits section for more information.

Introduction

"shown a flower": Patricia Donegan, trans., *Haiku Mind: 108 Poems to Cultivate Awareness and Open Your Heart* (Boston: Shambhala, 2008), 83.

"Unchurched, still I turn": *bear creek haiku,* no. 84 (2009).

Chapter One: The Heart of a Moment

"the distant mountain": David G. Lanoue, trans., from http://haikuguy.com/issa.

"new pond—": *A Path in the Garden* (Lake Oswego, Oreg.: Katsura Press, 2000), n.p.

"A haiku is ...": *Haiku,* vol. 1, *Eastern Culture* (Tokyo: Hokuseido Press), 243.

"dragonfly...": *A Path in the Garden.*

"I was sitting on a bench ...": "Interview with Christopher Herold," by Robert Wilson, in *Simply Haiku* 2 (March/April 2004): www.simplyhaiku.com/SHv2n2/features/Christopher_Herold.html.

"He has no home, yet": www.inthecourtyard.com, February 2009.

"Watching a man ...": E-mail message to author, February 5, 2009.

"Haiku brings us ...": *The Unswept Path: Contemporary American Haiku,* eds. John Brandi and Dennis Maloney, Companions for the Journey series, vol. 8 (Buffalo, N.Y.: White Pine Press, 2005), 85.

"summer grasses—": Donegan, trans., *Haiku Mind,* 9.

"haiku not only give us moments ...": William J. Higginson with Penny Harter, *The Haiku Handbook: How to Write, Share, and Teach Haiku* (Tokyo: Kodansha International, 1985), 6.

Chapter Two: A Simple Prayer

"Never more alone": The Haiku and Zen World of James W. Hackett, www.hacketthaiku.com. This and other haiku by James W. Hackett first appeared in slightly different form in *The Zen Haiku and Other Zen Poems of J. W. Hackett* (Tokyo: Japan Publications, 1983).

"Haiku are an expression of the joy of our reunion …": *Haiku*, vol. 1, 232.

"Brahman, or Ultimate Reality": *"Tat Tvam Asi,"* http://en.wikipedia.org/wiki/Tat_Tvam_Asi.

"the spirit, the truth": Donegan, trans., *Haiku Mind*, 137.

"Certainly the depth and breadth of life's Creation miracle …": "That Art Thou: Greater Nature," from The Haiku and Zen World of James W. Hackett, www.hacketthaiku.com/tat2titleGtNat25-33.html.

"Courage it is that endows us with the power …": *Haiku*, vol. 1, 236.

"weeding—": *Wisteria: A Journal of Haiku, Senryū, and Tanka* 12 (January 2009): 5.

"What isn't the imagination?": Conversation with author, May 4, 2009.

"So I keep trying gently …": Anne Lamott, *Bird by Bird: Some Instructions on Writing and Life* (New York: Pantheon Books, 1994), 99.

"Who are you trying to please?": Conversation with author, February 17, 2009.

Chapter Three: A Companionable Form

"ancient pond—": Donegan, trans., *Haiku Mind*, 117.

"waiting for you": Higginson with Harter, trans., *Haiku Handbook*, 182.

"Secret love—": *Tanka Light* (November 1999).

"Stumbling in the dark": www.inthecourtyard.com, January 2007.

"snowflakes": *The Heron's Nest* 9, no. 4 (2007): 76.

"sunrise …": *Frogpond: The Journal of the Haiku Society of America* 32, no. 2 (Spring/Summer 2009): 10.

"Any time a male pheasant …": E-mail message to author, July 13, 2009.

"There once was a man from Nantucket": The story of the limerick about the man from Nantucket can be found on numerous sites online, including www.yesterdaysisland.com/limerick/limerick.php.

"The quiet old pond ...": This is my rendering, after reading many different English translations of the poem.

"The basic tenet of Buddhism ...": Patricia Donegan and Yoshie Ishibashi, *Chiyo-ni: Woman Haiku Master* (Boston: Tuttle, 1998), 47.

"clear water is cool": Patricia Donegan, trans., from *The Unswept Path,* eds. Brandi and Maloney, 84.

"Haiku are most effective when in their element ...": E-mail message to author, February 17, 2009.

"A bitter morning": Haiku and Zen World of James W. Hackett.

"Learn of the pine from the pine ...": Quoted in Higginson with Harter, *Haiku Handbook,* 10.

"dark, dark night": *The Unswept Path,* eds. Brandi and Maloney, 120.

"what happens at this place ...": Quoted in Makoto Ueda, *Bashō and His Interpreters: Selected Hokku with Commentary* (Stanford, Calif.: Stanford University Press, 1995), 105.

"Recognize what is right in front of you ...": Stevan Davies, trans. and ann., *The Gospel of Thomas: Annotated and Explained,* SkyLight Illumination series (Woodstock, Vt.: SkyLight Paths, 2002), 7.

"If even one syllable ...": Letter to Takayama Biji, June 20, 1682, in Ueda, *Bashō and His Interpreters,* 80.

"disregard the old rules": Tom Lowenstein, *Haiku Inspirations: Poems and Meditations on Nature and Beauty* (London: Duncan Baird, 2006), 70.

Chapter Four: A Sense of Time and Place

"The time it takes—": *Haiku Moment,* ed. Bruce Ross (Boston: Tuttle, 1993).

"Behold! In the creation of the heavens ...": Yusuf Ali, trans., *The Qur'an and Sayings of Prophet Muhammad: Selections Annotated and Explained,* ann. and rev. by Sohaib N. Sultan, SkyLight Illuminations series (Woodstock, Vt.: SkyLight Paths, 2007), 3.

"once again": From *The Heron's Nest* 10, no. 3 (2008): 83.

"The *kigo* most likely has shaman/Shinto roots ...": Donegan and Ishibashi, *Chiyo-ni: Woman Haiku Master,* 65.

"spring wind—": *The Unswept Path,* eds. Brandi and Maloney, 99. This poem won first prize in the International Section of the Mainichi Haiku Contest in 1998.

"being able to appreciate … daily life …": "Haiku Winner Reflects on Poetry, Life," *Mainichi Newspaper,* July 1, 1998.

"genuine haiku moments …": E-mail message to author, May 31, 2009.

"This leaf too, with all": Haiku and Zen World of James W. Hackett.

"end of summer—": *Simply Haiku* 1, no. 5 (November 2003), www.simplyhaiku.com.

"winter's eve": *Wisteria: A Journal of Haiku, Senryū, and Tanka* 14 (July 2009): 17.

"circle of lamplight—": *The Heron's Nest* 9, no. 1 (2007): 13. This poem received the Heron's Nest Award.

"catching my breath": *Wisteria: A Journal of Haiku, Senryū, and Tanka* 12 (January 2009): 18.

Chapter Five: Inspired Conversations

"feel the truth of old poems": Quoted in *Bashō's Narrow Road: Spring and Autumn Passages,* trans. and ann. Hiroaki Sato (Berkeley, Calif.: Stone Bridge Press, 1996), 19.

"holy or sacred reading": Christine Valters Paintner and Lucy Wynkoop, *Lectio Divina: Contemplative Awakening and Awareness* (New York: Paulist Press, 2008), 1ff.

"A central aspect of the practice of listening …": Ibid., 18–19.

"The practice of *lectio divina* was an integral part of monastic life …": Ibid., 2. Guigo II, a twelfth-century Carthusian monk, first laid out the steps of *lectio divina* into a four-step process in his work *The Ladder of Monks.*

"the old fence post": *bear creek haiku,* no. 89.

Chapter Six: Haiku in Community

"letting go": Donegan, trans., *Haiku Mind,* 57.

"Every Particle in the World Is a Mirror": *The Essential Mystics,* ed. Andrew Harvey (San Francisco: HarperCollins, 1997), 163. This poem is excerpted from Shabistari's "The Rose Garden of Mystery," considered one of the greatest works of Persian Sufism.

Blush of the Beloved responds to "Every Particle in the World Is a Mirror": Written by Sally Marquis, Jane Ganas Long, Andrea

Bakke, Jamal Rahman, Chris Adams, Margaret D. McGee, Rick McClurg, Pauline Metcalfe, Su Phillips, and Maria Luiza C. Ramos at the Interfaith Community Church in Seattle, Washington, on January 24, 2009.

Passover Haiku: Written by Judith Glass Collins, Sarah Goldblatt, Margaret D. McGee, and Brian Rohr, and presented as part of the Bet Shira Congregation community Seder in Port Townsend, Washington, on April 10, 2009.

Chapter Seven: Haiku with Pictures or Prose

"He who binds to himself a joy": "Eternity," in *Complete Writings of William Blake,* ed. Geoffrey Keynes (London: Nonesuch Press, 1957).

the renowned woman haiku poet Chiyo-ni ...: Donegan and Ishibashi, *Chiyo-ni: Woman Haiku Master,* 35.

the "three perfections": Ibid., 50.

Chapter Eight: The Haiku Life

"Everything has a heart ...": Conversation with author, May 4, 2009.

"For me, haiku is more than a form ...": *The Unswept Path,* eds. Brandi and Maloney, 117.

"Make the universe your companion ...": Robert Hass, trans., *The Essential Haiku: Versions of Bashō, Buson, and Issa,* ed. Robert Hass (New York: HarperCollins, 1994), 233.

SUGGESTIONS FOR
FURTHER READING

Addiss, Stephen. *Haiga: Takebe Sōchō and the Haiku-Painting Tradition.* Honolulu, Hawaii/Richmond, Va.: Marsh Art Gallery and University of Richmond in association with the University of Hawai'i Press, 1995.

Bashō, Matsuo. *Bashō's Narrow Road: Spring and Autumn Passages.* Translated and annotated by Hiroaki Sato. Berkeley, Calif.: Stone Bridge Press, 1996.

———. *Narrow Road to the Interior.* Translated by Sam Hamill. Illustrated by Stephen Addiss. Boston: Shambhala, 2006.

Blake, William. *Blake: Complete Writings with Variant Readings.* Edited by Geoffrey Keynes. Oxford: Oxford University Press, 1966.

Blyth, R. H. *Haiku.* 4 vols. Tokyo: Hokuseido Press, 1949–52.

———. *A History of Haiku.* 2 vols. Tokyo: Hokuseido Press, 1963–64.

Bowers, Faubion, ed. *The Classic Tradition of Haiku: An Anthology.* Mineola, N.Y.: Dover, 1996.

Brandi, John, and Dennis Maloney, eds. *The Unswept Path: Contemporary American Haiku.* Companions for the Journey series, vol. 8. Buffalo, N.Y.: White Pine Press, 2005.

Chickerneo, Nancy Barrett. *Woman Spirit Awakening in Nature: Growing Into the Fullness of Who You Are.* Woodstock, Vt.: SkyLight Paths, 2008.

Davies, Stevan, trans. and ann. *The Gospel of Thomas: Annotated and Explained.* Woodstock, Vt.: SkyLight Paths, 2002.

Donegan, Patricia. *Haiku Mind: 108 Poems to Cultivate Awareness and Open Your Heart.* Boston: Shambhala, 2008.

Donegan, Patricia, and Yoshie Ishibashi. *Chiyo-ni: Woman Haiku Master.* Tokyo: Tuttle, 1998.

Gevirtz, Gila, ed. *The New American Haggadah*. Developed by Rabbi Mordecai M. Kaplan, Rabbi Eugene Kohn, and Rabbi Ira Eisenstein for the Jewish Reconstructionist Foundation. Springfield, N.J.: Behrman House, 1999.

Gurga, Lee. *Haiku: A Poet's Guide*. Lincoln, Ill.: Modern Haiku Press, 2003.

Hackett, James W. *The Zen Haiku and Other Zen Poems of J. W. Hackett*. Tokyo: Japan Publications, 1983.

Harvey, Andrew, ed. *The Essential Mystics: Selections from the World's Great Wisdom Traditions*. San Francisco: HarperCollins, 1997.

Hass, Robert, ed. *The Essential Haiku: Versions of Bashō, Buson, and Issa*. Hopewell, N.J.: Ecco Press, 1994.

Henderson, Harold G. *An Introduction to Haiku: An Anthology of Poems and Poets from Bashō to Shiki*. Garden City, N.Y.: Doubleday / Anchor, 1958.

Herold, Christopher. *A Path in the Garden*. Lake Oswego, Oreg.: Katsura Press, 2000.

Higginson, William J. *Haiku Seasons: Poetry of the Natural World*. Berkeley, Calif.: Stone Bridge Press, 2008.

———. *Haiku World: An International Poetry Almanac*. Tokyo: Kodansha International, 1996.

Higginson, William J., with Penny Harter. *The Haiku Handbook: How to Write, Share, and Teach Haiku*. Tokyo: Kodansha International, 1985.

Johnson, Cait. *Earth, Water, Fire, and Air: Essential Ways of Connecting to Spirit*. Woodstock, Vt.: SkyLight Paths, 2003.

Kacian, Jim, ed. *The Red Moon Anthology*. Multi-volume series. Berryville, Va.: Red Moon Press, 1997–.

Keene, Donald. *World within Walls: Japanese Literature of the Pre-Modern Era, 1600–1867*. New York: Columbia University Press, 1999.

Koren, Leonard. *Wabi-Sabi: For Artists, Designers, Poets and Philosophers*. Point Reyes, Calif.: Imperfect, 2008.

Lamott, Anne. *Bird by Bird: Some Instructions on Writing and Life*. New York: Anchor, 1995.

Lowenstein, Ted. *Haiku Inspirations: Poems and Meditations on Nature and Beauty*. London: Duncan Baird, 2006.

Mayall, Yolanda. *The Sumi-E Book*. New York: Watson-Guptill, 1989.

Reichhold, Jane. *Writing and Enjoying Haiku: A Hands-on Guide.* Tokyo: Kodansha International, 2002.

Ross, Bruce, ed. *Haiku Moment: An Anthology of Contemporary North American Haiku.* Boston: Tuttle, 1993.

Strand, Clark. *Seeds from a Birch Tree: Writing Haiku and the Spiritual Journey.* New York: Hyperion, 1998.

Sultan, Sohaib, ann. *The Qur'an and Sayings of Prophet Muhammad: Selections Annotated and Explained.* Translated by Yusuf Ali. Revised by Sohaib N. Sultan. Woodstock, Vt.: SkyLight Paths, 2007.

Suzuki, D. T. *Zen Buddhism: Selected Writings of D. T. Suzuki.* Edited by William Barrett. Garden City, N.Y.: Doubleday, 1956.

Ueda, Makoto, comp. and trans. *Bashō and His Interpreters: Selected Hokku with Commentary.* Stanford, Calif.: Stanford University Press, 1995.

————. *Matsuo Bashō: The Master Haiku Poet.* Tokyo: Kodansha International, 1982.

Valters Paintner, Christine, and Lucy Wynkoop. *Lectio Divina: Contemplative Awakening and Awareness.* New York: Paulist Press, 2008.

Van den Heuvel, Cor, ed. *The Haiku Anthology: Haiku and Senryū in English.* New York and London: W. W. Norton, 2000.

Wakan, Naomi Beth. *Haiku: One Breath Poetry.* Torrance, Calif.: Heian International, 1997.

CREDITS

I am grateful to the poets and publishers who have granted permission to reprint their work. Every attempt has been made to contact the authors or copyright holders of the works included in this book. The author would be pleased to hear from any copyright holders not acknowledged below.

I am also grateful to those who attended my workshops on writing haiku inspired by sacred texts and gave me permission to use the poems they wrote during the workshops. Their courage and openheartedness in sharing the process of writing haiku as a spiritual practice remains an inspiration to my own work. Many of their poems first appeared at www.inthecourtyard.com, and all are used with the permission of the individual authors.

Scriptural quotations are from the *New Revised Standard Version Bible,* copyright © 1989 by the Division of Christian Education of the National Council of the Churches of Christ in the USA. Used by permission. All rights reserved.

"ancient pond—" by Matsuo Bashō, trans. Patricia Donegan, from *Haiku Mind,* copyright © 2008 by Patricia Donegan. Reprinted by arrangement with Shambhala Publications, Inc., Boston, www.shambhala.com.

"Apricot dog dashes at," by Annika Wallendahl, copyright © 2009. Reprinted by permission of Annika Wallendahl.

"A bitter morning:" by James W. Hackett, www.hacketthaiku.com, copyright © 2004. Reprinted with permission of James W. Hackett.

"born of watermarks," by Sarah Goldblatt. Printed by permission of Sarah Goldblatt.

"catching my breath," by Linda Pilarski, from *Wisteria: A Journal of Haiku, Senryu, and Tanka* 12 (January 2009). Reprinted with permission of Linda Pilarski.

"circle of lamplight—" by Carolyn Hall, from *The Heron's Nest* 9:1 (2007). Reprinted with permission of Carolyn Hall.

"clear water is cool," by Chiyo-ni, trans. Patricia Donegan, from *The Unswept Path: Contemporary American Haiku,* eds. John Brandi and Dennis Maloney, copyright © 2005. Reprinted with permission of Patricia Donegan.

"cleave your wounded heart," by Andrea Bakke. Printed with permission of Andrea Bakke.

"Crooked sand castle," by Annika Wallendahl, copyright © 2009. Reprinted with permission of Annika Wallendahl.

"damp earth holding seed," by Rick McClurg. Printed with permission of Rick McClurg.

"dark, dark night," by Christopher Herold, from *The Unswept Path: Contemporary American Haiku,* eds. John Brandi and Dennis Maloney, copyright © 2005. Reprinted with permission of Christopher Herold.

"darkness," by Katrina Y. Spear. Printed with permission of Katrina Y. Spear.

"daybreak," by Margaret D. McGee, from *bear creek haiku* 89, copyright © 2009. Reprinted with permission of Margaret D. McGee.

"the distant mountain," by Kobayashi Issa, trans. David G. Lanoue, from http://haikuguy.com/issa. Reprinted with permission of David G. Lanoue.

"dragonfly ..." by Christopher Herold, from *A Path in the Garden,* copyright © 2000. Reprinted with permission of Christopher Herold.

"end of summer—" by Karma Tenzing Wangchuk, from *Simply Haiku* 1:5 (November 2003). Reprinted with permission of Karma Tenzing Wangchuk.

"Eternity," by William Blake, as reprinted in *The Complete Writings of William Blake,* ed. Geoffrey Keynes (London: Nonesuch Press, 1957). Public domain.

"First, give up being," by Margaret D. McGee from *Lectio*+Haiku at www.inthecourtyard.com (March 2007). Reprinted with permission of Margaret D. McGee.

"summer grasses—" by Matsuo Bashō, trans. Patricia Donegan, from *Haiku Mind,* copyright © 2008 by Patricia Donegan. Reprinted by arrangement with Shambhala Publications, Inc., Boston, www.shambhala.com.

"sun and shade play," by Margaret D. McGee, from www. inthecourtyard.com (July 2009). Reprinted with permission of Margaret D. McGee.

"sunrise ..." by Alice Frampton, from *Frogpond* 32:2 (June 2009). Reprinted with permission of Alice Frampton.

"there is no ending," by Doris H. Thurston. Printed by permission of Doris H. Thurston.

"This leaf too, with all," by James W. Hackett, www.hacketthaiku.com, copyright © 2004. Reprinted with permission of James W. Hackett.

"The time it takes—" by Lorraine Ellis Harr, copyright © 1993 by Lorraine Ellis Harr. Reprinted with permission of Lynn Haldeman and Martha Haldeman.

"trampled underfoot," by Valerie Johnstone. Printed with permission of Valerie Johnstone.

"Unchurched, still I turn," by Carl Mayfield, from *bear creek haiku* 84 (2009). Reprinted with permission of Carl Mayfield.

"up and born," by Judith Glass Collins. Printed with permission of Judith Glass Collins.

"waiting for you," by Princess Nukuda, trans. William J. Higginson with Penny Harter, copyright © 1989. Reprinted by permission of Penny Harter.

"weeding—" by Deborah A. Baker, from *Wisteria: A Journal of Haiku, Senryu, and Tanka* 12 (January 2009). Reprinted with permission of Deborah A. Baker.

"winter's eve," by Margaret D. McGee, from *Wisteria: A Journal of Haiku, Senryu, and Tanka* 14 (July 2009). Reprinted with permission of Margaret D. McGee.

"Wonders within wonders!" by Jamal Rahman. Printed with permission of Jamal Rahman.

INDEX OF PRACTICES

INDEX OF POETS

Global Spiritual Perspectives

Spiritual Perspectives on America's Role as Superpower
by the Editors at SkyLight Paths

Are we the world's good neighbor or a global bully? From a spiritual perspective, what are America's responsibilities as the only remaining superpower? Contributors:

Dr. Beatrice Bruteau • Dr. Joan Brown Campbell • Tony Campolo • Rev. Forrest Church • Lama Surya Das • Matthew Fox • Kabir Helminski • Thich Nhat Hanh • Eboo Patel • Abbot M. Basil Pennington, ocso • Dennis Prager • Rosemary Radford Ruether • Wayne Teasdale • Rev. William McD. Tully • Rabbi Arthur Waskow • John Wilson

5½ x 8½, 256 pp, Quality PB, 978-1-893361-81-2 **$16.95**

Spiritual Perspectives on Globalization, 2nd Edition
Making Sense of Economic and Cultural Upheaval
by Ira Rifkin; Foreword by Dr. David Little, Harvard Divinity School

What is globalization? Surveys the religious landscape. Includes a new Discussion Guide designed for group use.

5½ x 8½, 256 pp, Quality PB, 978-1-59473-045-0 **$16.99**

Hinduism / Vedanta

The Four Yogas
A Guide to the Spiritual Paths of Action, Devotion, Meditation and Knowledge
by Swami Adiswarananda
6 x 9, 320 pp, Quality PB, 978-1-59473-223-2 **$19.99**; HC, 978-1-59473-143-3 **$29.99**

Meditation & Its Practices
A Definitive Guide to Techniques and Traditions of Meditation in Yoga and Vedanta
by Swami Adiswarananda 6 x 9, 504 pp, Quality PB, 978-1-59473-105-1 **$24.99**

The Spiritual Quest and the Way of Yoga: The Goal, the Journey and the Milestones
by Swami Adiswarananda 6 x 9, 288 pp, HC, 978-1-59473-113-6 **$29.99**

Sri Ramakrishna, the Face of Silence
by Swami Nikhilananda and Dhan Gopal Mukerji
Edited with an Introduction by Swami Adiswarananda; Foreword by Dhan Gopal Mukerji II
Classic biographies present the life and thought of Sri Ramakrishna.
6 x 9, 352 pp, Quality PB, 978-1-59473-233-1 **$21.99**; HC, 978-1-59473-115-0 **$29.99**

Sri Sarada Devi, The Holy Mother: Her Teachings and Conversations
Translated with Notes by Swami Nikhilananda; Edited with an Introduction by Swami Adiswarananda
6 x 9, 288 pp, HC, 978-1-59473-070-2 **$29.99**

The Vedanta Way to Peace and Happiness *by Swami Adiswarananda*
6 x 9, 240 pp, Quality PB, 978-1-59473-180-8 **$18.99**

Vivekananda, World Teacher: His Teachings on the Spiritual Unity of Humankind
Edited and with an Introduction by Swami Adiswarananda
6 x 9, 272 pp, Quality PB, 978-1-59473-210-2 **$21.99**

Sikhism

The First Sikh Spiritual Master
Timeless Wisdom from the Life and Teachings of Guru Nanak *by Harish Dhillon*
Tells the story of a unique spiritual leader who showed a gentle, peaceful path to God-realization while highlighting Guru Nanak's quest for tolerance and compassion. 6 x 9, 192 pp, Quality PB, 978-1-59473-209-6 **$16.99**

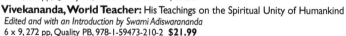

Or phone, fax, mail or e-mail to: SKYLIGHT PATHS Publishing
An imprint of Turner Publishing Company
4507 Charlotte Avenue • Suite 100 • Nashville, TN 37209
Tel: (615) 255-2665 • www.skylightpaths.com
Prices subject to change.

Midrash Fiction / Folktales

Abraham's Bind & Other Bible Tales of Trickery, Folly, Mercy and Love *by Michael J. Caduto*
New retellings of episodes in the lives of familiar biblical characters explore relevant life lessons.
6 x 9, 224 pp, HC, 978-1-59473-186-0 **$19.99**

Daughters of the Desert: Stories of Remarkable Women from Christian, Jewish and Muslim Traditions *by Claire Rudolf Murphy, Meghan Nuttall Sayres, Mary Cronk Farrell, Sarah Conover and Betsy Wharton*
Breathes new life into the old tales of our female ancestors in faith. Uses traditional scriptural passages as starting points, then with vivid detail fills in historical context and place. Chapters reveal the voices of Sarah, Hagar, Huldah, Esther, Salome, Mary Magdalene, Lydia, Khadija, Fatima and many more. Historical fiction ideal for readers of all ages. Quality paperback includes reader's discussion guide.
5½ x 8½, 192 pp, Quality PB, 978-1-59473-106-8 **$14.99**
HC, 192 pp, 978-1-893361-72-0 **$19.95**

The Triumph of Eve & Other Subversive Bible Tales
by Matt Biers-Ariel
Many people were taught and remember only a one-dimensional Bible. These engaging retellings are the antidote to this—they're witty, often hilarious, always profound, and invite you to grapple with questions and issues that are often hidden in the original text.
5½ x 8½, 192 pp, Quality PB, 978-1-59473-176-1 **$14.99**

Also avail.: **The Triumph of Eve Teacher's Guide**
8½ x 11, 44 pp, PB, 978-1-59473-152-5 **$8.99**

Wisdom in the Telling
Finding Inspiration and Grace in Traditional Folktales and Myths Retold
by Lorraine Hartin-Gelardi
6 x 9, 224 pp, HC, 978-1-59473-185-3 **$19.99**

Religious Etiquette / Reference

How to Be a Perfect Stranger, 4th Edition: The Essential Religious Etiquette Handbook *Edited by Stuart M. Matlins and Arthur J. Magida*
The indispensable guidebook to help the well-meaning guest when visiting other people's religious ceremonies. A straightforward guide to the rituals and celebrations of the major religions and denominations in the United States and Canada from the perspective of an interested guest of any other faith, based on information obtained from authorities from each religion. Belongs in every living room, library and office. Covers:
African American Methodist Churches • Assemblies of God • Bahá'í • Baptist • Buddhist • Christian Church (Disciples of Christ) • Christian Science (Church of Christ, Scientist) • Churches of Christ • Episcopalian and Anglican • Hindu • Islam • Jehovah's Witnesses • Jewish • Lutheran • Mennonite/Amish • Methodist • Mormon (Church of Jesus Christ of Latter-day Saints) • Native American/First Nations • Orthodox Churches • Pentecostal Church of God • Presbyterian • Quaker (Religious Society of Friends) • Reformed Church in America/Canada • Roman Catholic • Seventh-day Adventist • Sikh • Unitarian Universalist • United Church of Canada • United Church of Christ
6 x 9, 432 pp, Quality PB, 978-1-59473-140-2 **$19.99**

The Perfect Stranger's Guide to Funerals and Grieving Practices: A Guide to Etiquette in Other People's Religious Ceremonies *Edited by Stuart M. Matlins*
6 x 9, 240 pp, Quality PB, 978-1-893361-20-1 **$16.95**

The Perfect Stranger's Guide to Wedding Ceremonies: A Guide to Etiquette in Other People's Religious Ceremonies *Edited by Stuart M. Matlins*
6 x 9, 208 pp, Quality PB, 978-1-893361-19-5 **$16.95**

Children's Spirituality

Adam and Eve's First Sunset: God's New Day
by Sandy Eisenberg Sasso; Full-color illus. by Joani Keller Rothenberg 9 x 12, 32 pp, Full-color illus., HC, 978-1-58023-177-0 **$17.95** *For ages 4 & up (A book from Jewish Lights, SkyLight Paths' sister imprint)*

Because Nothing Looks Like God
by Lawrence and Karen Kushner; Full-color illus. by Dawn W. Majewski
Real-life examples of happiness and sadness introduce children to the possibilities of spiritual life. 11 x 8½, 32 pp, HC, Full-color illus., 978-1-58023-092-6 **$17.99**
For ages 4 & up (A book from Jewish Lights, SkyLight Paths' sister imprint)
Also available: **Teacher's Guide,** 8½ x 11, 22 pp, PB, 978-1-58023-140-4 **$6.95** *For ages 5–8*

But God Remembered: Stories of Women from Creation to the Promised Land *by Sandy Eisenberg Sasso; Full-color illus. by Bethanne Andersen*
A fascinating collection of four different stories of women only briefly mentioned in biblical tradition and religious texts.
9 x 12, 32 pp, Full-color illus., Quality PB, 978-1-58023-372-9 **$12.99**; HC, 978-1-879045-43-9 **$16.95**
For ages 8 & up (A book from Jewish Lights, SkyLight Paths' sister imprint)

Cain & Abel: Finding the Fruits of Peace
by Sandy Eisenberg Sasso; Full-color illus. by Joani Keller Rothenberg
A sensitive recasting of the ancient tale shows we have the power to deal with anger in positive ways. "Editor's Choice"—American Library Association's *Booklist*
9 x 12, 32 pp, HC, Full-color illus., 978-1-58023-123-7 **$16.95** *For ages 5 & up (A book from Jewish Lights, SkyLight Paths' sister imprint)*

Does God Hear My Prayer?
by August Gold; Full-color photos by Diane Hardy Waller
Introduces preschoolers and young readers to prayer and how it helps them express their own emotions. 10 x 8½, 32 pp, Quality PB, Full-color photo illus., 978-1-59473-102-0 **$8.99**

The 11th Commandment: Wisdom from Our Children *by The Children of America*
"If there were an Eleventh Commandment, what would it be?" Children of many religious denominations across America answer this question—in their own drawings and words. "A rare book of spiritual celebration for all people, of all ages, for all time." —*Bookviews* 8 x 10, 48 pp, HC, Full-color illus., 978-1-879045-46-0 **$16.95**
For all ages (A book from Jewish Lights, SkyLight Paths' sister imprint)

For Heaven's Sake *by Sandy Eisenberg Sasso; Full-color illus. by Kathryn Kunz Finney*
What heaven is and where to find it. 9 x 12, 32 pp, HC, Full-color illus., 978-1-58023-054-4 **$16.95** *For ages 4 & up (A book from Jewish Lights, SkyLight Paths' sister imprint)*

God in Between *by Sandy Eisenberg Sasso; Full-color illus. by Sally Sweetland*
A magical, mythical tale that teaches that God can be found where we are.
9 x 12, 32 pp, HC, Full-color illus., 978-1-879045-86-6 **$16.95** *For ages 4 & up (A book from Jewish Lights, SkyLight Paths' sister imprint)*

God's Paintbrush: Special 10th Anniversary Edition
Invites children of all faiths and backgrounds to encounter God through moments in their own lives. 11 x 8½, 32 pp, Full-color illus., HC, 978-1-58023-195-4 **$17.95** *For ages 4 & up*
Also available: **I Am God's Paintbrush** (A Board Book)
by Sandy Eisenberg Sasso; Full-color illus. by Annette Compton
5 x 5, 24 pp, Board Book, Full-color illus., 978-1-59473-265-2 **$7.99** *For ages 0–4*
Also available: **God's Paintbrush Teacher's Guide** 8½ x 11, 32 pp, PB, 978-1-879045-57-6 **$8.95**
God's Paintbrush Celebration Kit
A Spiritual Activity Kit for Teachers and Students of All Faiths, All Backgrounds
Additional activity sheets available:
8-Student Activity Sheet Pack (40 sheets/5 sessions), 978-1-58023-058-2 **$19.95**
Single-Student Activity Sheet Pack (5 sessions), 978-1-58023-059-9 **$3.95**

Children's Spirituality

Remembering My Grandparent: A Kid's Own Grief Workbook in the Christian Tradition *by Nechama Liss-Levinson, PhD, and Rev. Molly Phinney Baskette, MDiv* 8 x 10, 48 pp, 2-color text, HC, 978-1-59473-212-6 **$16.99** *For ages 7–13*

Does God Ever Sleep? *by Joan Sauro, CSJ; Full-color photos*
A charming nighttime reminder that God is always present in our lives.
10 x 8½, 32 pp, Quality PB, Full-color photos, 978-1-59473-110-5 **$8.99** *For ages 3–6*

Does God Forgive Me? *by August Gold; Full-color photos by Diane Hardy Waller*
Gently shows how God forgives all that we do if we are truly sorry.
10 x 8½, 32 pp, Quality PB, Full-color photos, 978-1-59473-142-6 **$8.99** *For ages 3–6*

God Said Amen *by Sandy Eisenberg Sasso; Full-color illus. by Avi Katz*
A warm and inspiring tale of two kingdoms that shows us that we need only reach out to each other to find the answers to our prayers.
9 x 12, 32 pp, HC, Full-color illus., 978-1-58023-080-3 **$16.95**
For ages 4 & up (A book from Jewish Lights, SkyLight Paths' sister imprint)

How Does God Listen? *by Kay Lindahl; Full-color photos by Cynthia Maloney*
How do we know when God is listening to us? Children will find the answers to these questions as they engage their senses while the story unfolds, learning how God listens in the wind, waves, clouds, hot chocolate, perfume, our tears and our laughter.
10 x 8½, 32 pp, Quality PB, Full-color photos, 978-1-59473-084-9 **$8.99** *For ages 3–6*

In God's Hands *by Lawrence Kushner and Gary Schmidt; Full-color illus. by Matthew J. Baeck*
9 x 12, 32 pp, Full-color illus., HC, 978-1-58023-224-1 **$16.99** *For ages 5 & up (A book from Jewish Lights, SkyLight Paths' sister imprint)*

In God's Name *by Sandy Eisenberg Sasso; Full-color illus. by Phoebe Stone*
Like an ancient myth in its poetic text and vibrant illustrations, this award-winning modern fable about the search for God's name celebrates the diversity and, at the same time, the unity of all the people of the world.
9 x 12, 32 pp, HC, Full-color illus., 978-1-879045-26-2 **$16.99**
For ages 4 & up (A book from Jewish Lights, SkyLight Paths' sister imprint)

Also available in Spanish: **El nombre de Dios**
9 x 12, 32 pp, HC, Full-color illus., 978-1-893361-63-8 **$16.95**

In Our Image: God's First Creatures
by Nancy Sohn Swartz; Full-color illus. by Melanie Hall
A playful new twist on the Genesis story—from the perspective of the animals. Celebrates the interconnectedness of nature and the harmony of all living things.
9 x 12, 32 pp, HC, Full-color illus., 978-1-879045-99-6 **$16.95**
For ages 4 & up (A book from Jewish Lights, SkyLight Paths' sister imprint)

Noah's Wife: The Story of Naamah
by Sandy Eisenberg Sasso; Full-color illus. by Bethanne Andersen
This new story, based on an ancient text, opens readers' religious imaginations to new ideas about the well-known story of the Flood. When God tells Noah to bring the animals of the world onto the ark, God also calls on Naamah, Noah's wife, to save each plant on Earth.
9 x 12, 32 pp, HC, Full-color illus., 978-1-58023-134-3 **$16.95**
For ages 4 & up (A book from Jewish Lights, SkyLight Paths' sister imprint)

Also available: **Naamah:** Noah's Wife (A Board Book)
by Sandy Eisenberg Sasso; Full-color illus. by Bethanne Andersen
5 x 5, 24 pp, Board Book, Full-color illus., 978-1-893361-56-0 **$7.99** *For ages 0–4*

Where Does God Live? *by August Gold and Matthew J. Perlman*
Using simple, everyday examples that children can relate to, this colorful book helps young readers develop a personal understanding of God.
10 x 8½, 32 pp, Quality PB, Full-color photo illus., 978-1-893361-39-3 **$8.99** *For ages 3–6*

Children's Spirituality—Board Books

Adam and Eve's New Day (A Board Book)
by Sandy Eisenberg Sasso; Full-color illus. by Joani Keller Rothenberg
A lesson in hope for every child who has worried about what comes next. Abridged from *Adam and Eve's First Sunset*.
5 x 5, 24 pp, Full-color illus., Board Book, 978-1-59473-205-8 **$7.99** *For ages 0–4*

How Did the Animals Help God? (A Board Book)
by Nancy Sohn Swartz; Full-color illus. by Melanie Hall
Abridged from *In Our Image*, God asks all of nature to offer gifts to humankind— with a promise that they will care for creation in return.
5 x 5, 24 pp, Board Book, Full-color illus., 978-1-59473-044-3 **$7.99** *For ages 0–4*

Where Is God? (A Board Book) *by Lawrence and Karen Kushner; Full-color illus. by Dawn W. Majewski* A gentle way for young children to explore how God is with us every day, in every way. Abridged from *Because Nothing Looks Like God*.
5 x 5, 24 pp, Board Book, Full-color illus., 978-1-893361-17-1 **$7.99** *For ages 0–4*

What Does God Look Like? (A Board Book)
by Lawrence and Karen Kushner; Full-color illus. by Dawn W. Majewski
A simple way for young children to explore the ways that we "see" God. Abridged from *Because Nothing Looks Like God*.
5 x 5, 24 pp, Board Book, Full-color illus., 978-1-893361-23-2 **$7.99** *For ages 0–4*

How Does God Make Things Happen? (A Board Book)
by Lawrence and Karen Kushner; Full-color illus. by Dawn W. Majewski
A charming invitation for young children to explore how God makes things happen in our world. Abridged from *Because Nothing Looks Like God*.
5 x 5, 24 pp, Board Book, Full-color illus., 978-1-893361-24-9 **$7.99** *For ages 0–4*

What Is God's Name? (A Board Book)
by Sandy Eisenberg Sasso; Full-color illus. by Phoebe Stone
Everyone and everything in the world has a name. What is God's name? Abridged from the award-winning *In God's Name*.
5 x 5, 24 pp, Board Book, Full-color illus., 978-1-893361-10-2 **$7.99** *For ages 0–4*

What You Will See Inside ...

This important new series of books, each with many full-color photos, is designed to show children ages 6 and up the Who, What, When, Where, Why and How of traditional houses of worship, liturgical celebrations, and rituals of different world faiths, empowering them to respect and understand their own religious traditions—and those of their friends and neighbors.

What You Will See Inside a Catholic Church
by Reverend Michael Keane; Foreword by Robert J. Keeley, EdD
Full-color photos by Aaron Pepis
8½ x 10½, 32 pp, Full-color photos, HC, 978-1-893361-54-6 **$17.95**

Also available in Spanish: **Lo que se puede ver dentro de una iglesia católica**
8½ x 10½, 32 pp, Full-color photos, HC, 978-1-893361-66-9 **$16.95**

What You Will See Inside a Hindu Temple
by Dr. Mahendra Jani and Dr. Vandana Jani; Full-color photos by Neirah Bhargava and Vijay Dave
8½ x 10½, 32 pp, Full-color photos, HC, 978-1-59473-116-7 **$17.99**

What You Will See Inside a Mosque
by Aisha Karen Khan; Full-color photos by Aaron Pepis
8¼ x 10¼, 32 pp, Full-color photos, Quality PB, 978-1-59473-257-7 **$12.99**; HC, 978-1-893361-60-7 **$16.95**

What You Will See Inside a Synagogue
by Rabbi Lawrence A. Hoffman and Dr. Ron Wolfson; Full-color photos by Bill Aron
8¼ x 10¼, 32 pp, Full-color photos, Quality PB, 978-1-59473-256-0 **$12.99**; HC, 978-1-59473-012-2 **$17.99**

Judaism / Christianity / Interfaith

Getting to the Heart of Interfaith: The Eye-Opening, Hope-Filled
Friendship of a Pastor, a Rabbi and a Sheikh
by Pastor Don Mackenzie, Rabbi Ted Falcon and Sheikh Jamal Rahman
Offers many insights and encouragements for individuals and groups who want to tap
into the promise of interfaith dialogue. 6 x 9, 192 pp, Quality PB, 978-1-59473-263-8 **$16.99**

How to Do Good and Avoid Evil: A Global Ethic from the Sources of
Judaism *by Hans Küng and Rabbi Walter Homolka; Translated by Rev. Dr. John Bowden*
Explores how the principles of a global ethic can be found in Judaism.
6 x 9, 224 pp, HC, 978-1-59473-255-3 **$19.99**

Hearing the Call across Traditions: Readings on Faith and Service
Edited by Adam Davis; Foreword by Eboo Patel Explores the connections between faith,
service, and social justice through the prose, verse, and sacred texts of the
world's great faith traditions. 6 x 9, 352 pp, HC, 978-1-59473-264-5 **$29.99**

The Jewish Approach to Repairing the World (*Tikkun Olam*)
A Brief Introduction for Christians *by Rabbi Elliot N. Dorff, PhD, with Reverend Cory Willson*
A window into the Jewish idea of responsibility to care for the world.
5½ x 8½, 256 pp, Quality PB, 978-1-58023-349-1 **$16.99** *(A book from Jewish Lights, SkyLight
Paths' sister imprint)*

Modern Jews Engage the New Testament: Enhancing Jewish Well-
Being in a Christian Environment *by Rabbi Michael J. Cook, PhD*
A look at the dynamics of the New Testament. 6 x 9, 416 pp, HC, 978-1-58023-313-2
$29.99 *(A book from Jewish Lights, SkyLight Paths' sister imprint)*

The Changing Christian World: A Brief Introduction for Jews
by Rabbi Leonard A. Schoolman 5½ x 8½, 176 pp, Quality PB, 978-1-58023-344-6 **$16.99**
(A book from Jewish Lights, SkyLight Paths' sister imprint)

Christians and Jews in Dialogue: Learning in the Presence of the Other
by Mary C. Boys and Sara S. Lee; Foreword by Dorothy C. Bass
6 x 9, 240 pp, HC, 978-1-59473-144-0 **$21.99**

Disaster Spiritual Care: Practical Clergy Responses to Community, Regional and
National Tragedy *Edited by Rabbi Stephen B. Roberts, BCJC, & Rev. Willard W.C. Ashley, Sr., DMin, DH*
6 x 9, 384 pp, HC, 978-1-59473-240-9 **$40.00**

Interactive Faith: The Essential Interreligious Community-Building Handbook
Edited by Rev. Bud Heckman 6 x 9, 304 pp, HC, 978-1-59473-237-9 **$40.00**

The Jewish Approach to God: A Brief Introduction for Christians *by Rabbi Neil Gillman*
5½ x 8½, 192 pp, Quality PB, 978-1-58023-190-9 **$16.95** *(A book from Jewish Lights, SkyLight
Paths' sister imprint)*

The Jewish Connection to Israel, the Promised Land: A Brief Introduction for
Christians *by Rabbi Eugene Korn, PhD* 5½ x 8½, 192 pp, Quality PB, 978-1-58023-318-7 **$14.99**
(A book from Jewish Lights, SkyLight Paths' sister imprint)

Jewish Holidays: A Brief Introduction for Christians *by Rabbi Kerry M. Olitzky and
Rabbi Daniel Judson* 5½ x 8½, 176 pp, Quality PB, 978-1-58023-302-6 **$16.99**
(A book from Jewish Lights, SkyLight Paths' sister imprint)

Jewish Ritual: A Brief Introduction for Christians
by Rabbi Kerry M. Olitzky and Rabbi Daniel Judson 5½ x 8½, 144 pp, Quality PB, 978-1-58023-210-4 **$14.99**
(A book from Jewish Lights, SkyLight Paths' sister imprint)

Jewish Spirituality: A Brief Introduction for Christians *by Rabbi Lawrence Kushner*
5½ x 8½, 112 pp, Quality PB, 978-1-58023-150-3 **$12.95** *(A book from Jewish Lights, SkyLight
Paths' sister imprint)*

A Jewish Understanding of the New Testament *by Rabbi Samuel Sandmel;
new Preface by Rabbi David Sandmel* 5½ x 8½, 368 pp, Quality PB, 978-1-59473-048-1 **$19.99**

Talking about God: Exploring the Meaning of Religious Life with Kierkegaard, Buber,
Tillich and Heschel *by Daniel F. Polish, PhD* 6 x 9, 176 pp, HC, 978-1-59473-230-0 **$21.99**

We Jews and Jesus: Exploring Theological Differences for Mutual Understanding
by Rabbi Samuel Sandmel; new Preface by Rabbi David Sandmel A Classic Reprint
6 x 9, 192 pp, Quality PB, 978-1-59473-208-9 **$16.99**

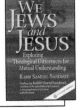

Sacred Texts—SkyLight Illuminations Series

Offers today's spiritual seeker an accessible entry into the great classic texts of the world's spiritual traditions. Each classic is presented in an accessible translation, with facing pages of guided commentary from experts, giving you the keys you need to understand the history, context and meaning of the text. This series enables you, whatever your background, to experience and understand classic spiritual texts directly, and to make them a part of your life.

CHRISTIANITY

The End of Days: Essential Selections from Apocalyptic Texts—
Annotated & Explained *Annotation by Robert G. Clouse*
Helps you understand the complex Christian visions of the end of the world.
5½ x 8½, 224 pp, Quality PB, 978-1-59473-170-9 **$16.99**

The Hidden Gospel of Matthew: Annotated & Explained
Translation & Annotation by Ron Miller
Takes you deep into the text cherished around the world to discover the words and events that have the strongest connection to the historical Jesus.
5½ x 8½, 272 pp, Quality PB, 978-1-59473-038-2 **$16.99**

The Infancy Gospels of Jesus: Apocryphal Tales from the Childhoods of Mary and Jesus—Annotated & Explained *Stevan Davies; Foreword by A. Edward Siecienski*
A startling presentation of the early lives of Mary, Jesus, and other biblical figures that will amuse and surprise you. 5½ x 8½, 176 pp, Quality PB Original, 978-1-59473-258-4 **$16.99**

The Lost Sayings of Jesus: Teachings from Ancient Christian, Jewish, Gnostic and Islamic Sources—Annotated & Explained
Translation & Annotation by Andrew Phillip Smith; Foreword by Stephan A. Hoeller
This collection of more than three hundred sayings depicts Jesus as a Wisdom teacher who speaks to people of all faiths as a mystic and spiritual master.
5½ x 8½, 240 pp, Quality PB, 978-1-59473-172-3 **$16.99**

Philokalia: The Eastern Christian Spiritual Texts—Selections Annotated & Explained *Annotation by Allyne Smith; Translation by G. E. H. Palmer, Phillip Sherrard and Bishop Kallistos Ware*
The first approachable introduction to the wisdom of the Philokalia, which is the classic text of Eastern Christian spirituality.
5½ x 8½, 240 pp, Quality PB, 978-1-59473-103-7 **$16.99**

The Sacred Writings of Paul: Selections Annotated & Explained
Translation & Annotation by Ron Miller
Explores the apostle Paul's core message of spiritual equality, freedom and joy.
5½ x 8½, 224 pp, Quality PB, 978-1-59473-213-3 **$16.99**

Sex Texts from the Bible: Selections Annotated & Explained
Translation & Annotation by Teresa J. Hornsby; Foreword by Amy-Jill Levine
Offers surprising insight into our modern sexual lives.
5½ x 8½, 208 pp, Quality PB, 978-1-59473-217-1 **$16.99**

Spiritual Writings on Mary: Annotated & Explained
Annotation by Mary Ford-Grabowsky; Foreword by Andrew Harvey
Examines the role of Mary, the mother of Jesus, as a source of inspiration in history and in life today. 5½ x 8½, 288 pp, Quality PB, 978-1-59473-001-6 **$16.99**

The Way of a Pilgrim: The Jesus Prayer Journey—Annotated & Explained
Translation & Annotation by Gleb Pokrovsky; Foreword by Andrew Harvey
This classic of Russian spirituality is the delightful account of one man who sets out to learn the prayer of the heart, also known as the "Jesus prayer."
5½ x 8½, 160 pp, Illus., Quality PB, 978-1-893361-31-7 **$14.95**

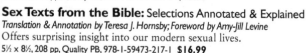

Sacred Texts—cont.

MORMONISM

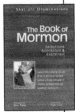

The Book of Mormon: Selections Annotated & Explained
Annotation by Jana Riess; Foreword by Phyllis Tickle
Explores the sacred epic that is cherished by more than twelve million members of the LDS church as the keystone of their faith.
5½ x 8½, 272 pp, Quality PB, 978-1-59473-076-4 **$16.99**

NATIVE AMERICAN

Native American Stories of the Sacred: Annotated & Explained
Retold & Annotated by Evan T. Pritchard
Intended for more than entertainment, these teaching tales contain elegantly simple illustrations of time-honored truths.
5½ x 8½, 272 pp, Quality PB, 978-1-59473-112-9 **$16.99**

GNOSTICISM

Gnostic Writings on the Soul: Annotated & Explained
Translation & Annotation by Andrew Phillip Smith; Foreword by Stephan A. Hoeller
Reveals the inspiring ways your soul can remember and return to its unique, divine purpose.
5½ x 8½, 144 pp, Quality PB, 978-1-59473-220-1 **$16.99**

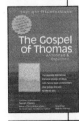

The Gospel of Philip: Annotated & Explained
Translation & Annotation by Andrew Phillip Smith; Foreword by Stevan Davies
Reveals otherwise unrecorded sayings of Jesus and fragments of Gnostic mythology.
5½ x 8½, 160 pp, Quality PB, 978-1-59473-111-2 **$16.99**

The Gospel of Thomas: Annotated & Explained
Translation & Annotation by Stevan Davies Sheds new light on the origins of Christianity and portrays Jesus as a wisdom-loving sage.
5½ x 8½, 192 pp, Quality PB, 978-1-893361-45-4 **$16.99**

The Secret Book of John: The Gnostic Gospel—Annotated & Explained
Translation & Annotation by Stevan Davies The most significant and influential text of the ancient Gnostic religion.
5½ x 8½, 208 pp, Quality PB, 978-1-59473-082-5 **$16.99**

JUDAISM

The Divine Feminine in Biblical Wisdom Literature
Selections Annotated & Explained
Translation & Annotation by Rabbi Rami Shapiro; Foreword by Rev. Cynthia Bourgeault, PhD
Uses the Hebrew books of Psalms, Proverbs, Song of Songs, Ecclesiastes and Job, Wisdom literature and the Wisdom of Solomon to clarify who Wisdom is.
5½ x 8½, 240 pp, Quality PB, 978-1-59473-109-9 **$16.99**

Ethics of the Sages: *Pirke Avot*—Annotated & Explained
Translation & Annotation by Rabbi Rami Shapiro Clarifies the ethical teachings of the early Rabbis. 5½ x 8½, 192 pp, Quality PB, 978-1-59473-207-2 **$16.99**

Hasidic Tales: Annotated & Explained
Translation & Annotation by Rabbi Rami Shapiro
Introduces the legendary tales of the impassioned Hasidic rabbis, presenting them as stories rather than as parables. 5½ x 8½, 240 pp, Quality PB, 978-1-893361-86-7 **$16.95**

The Hebrew Prophets: Selections Annotated & Explained
Translation & Annotation by Rabbi Rami Shapiro; Foreword by Zalman M. Schachter-Shalomi
Focuses on the central themes covered by all the Hebrew prophets.
5½ x 8½, 224 pp, Quality PB, 978-1-59473-037-5 **$16.99**

Zohar: Annotated & Explained *Translation & Annotation by Daniel C. Matt*
The best-selling author of *The Essential Kabbalah* brings together in one place the most important teachings of the Zohar, the canonical text of Jewish mystical tradition.
5½ x 8½, 176 pp, Quality PB, 978-1-893361-51-5 **$15.99**

Sacred Texts—cont.

ISLAM

The Qur'an and Sayings of Prophet Muhammad
Selections Annotated & Explained

Annotation by Sohaib N. Sultan; Translation by Yusuf Ali; Revised by Sohaib N. Sultan
Foreword by Jane I. Smith

Explores how the timeless wisdom of the Qur'an can enrich your own spiritual journey.

5½ x 8½, 256 pp, Quality PB, 978-1-59473-222-5 **$16.99**

Rumi and Islam: Selections from His Stories, Poems, and Discourses—
Annotated & Explained

Translation & Annotation by Ibrahim Gamard

Focuses on Rumi's place within the Sufi tradition of Islam, providing insight into the mystical side of the religion.

5½ x 8½, 240 pp, Quality PB, 978-1-59473-002-3 **$15.99**

EASTERN RELIGIONS

The Art of War—Spirituality for Conflict
Annotated & Explained

by Sun Tzu; Annotation by Thomas Huynh; Translation by Thomas Huynh and the Editors at Sonshi.com; Foreword by Marc Benioff; Preface by Thomas Cleary

Highlights principles that encourage a perceptive and spiritual approach to conflict.

5½ x 8½, 256 pp, Quality PB, 978-1-59473-244-7 **$16.99**

Bhagavad Gita: Annotated & Explained

Translation by Shri Purohit Swami; Annotation by Kendra Crossen Burroughs

Explains references and philosophical terms, shares the interpretations of famous spiritual leaders and scholars, and more.

5½ x 8½, 192 pp, Quality PB, 978-1-893361-28-7 **$16.95**

Dhammapada: Annotated & Explained

Translation by Max Müller and revised by Jack Maguire; Annotation by Jack Maguire

Contains all of Buddhism's key teachings.

5½ x 8½, 160 pp, b/w photos, Quality PB, 978-1-893361-42-3 **$14.95**

Selections from the Gospel of Sri Ramakrishna
Annotated & Explained

Translation by Swami Nikhilananda; Annotation by Kendra Crossen Burroughs

Introduces the fascinating world of the Indian mystic and the universal appeal of his message.

5½ x 8½, 240 pp, b/w photos, Quality PB, 978-1-893361-46-1 **$16.95**

Tao Te Ching: Annotated & Explained

Translation & Annotation by Derek Lin; Foreword by Lama Surya Das

Introduces an Eastern classic in an accessible, poetic and completely original way.

5½ x 8½, 192 pp, Quality PB, 978-1-59473-204-1 **$16.99**

STOICISM

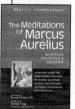

The Meditations of Marcus Aurelius
Selections Annotated & Explained

Annotation by Russell McNeil, PhD; Translation by George Long; Revised by Russell McNeil, PhD

Offers insightful and engaging commentary into the historical background of Stoicism.

5½ x 8½, 288 pp, Quality PB, 978-1-59473-236-2 **$16.99**

Spiritual Biography / Reference

Hearing the Call across Traditions
Readings on Faith and Service
Edited by Adam Davis; Foreword by Eboo Patel
Explores the connections between faith, service, and social justice through the prose, verse, and sacred texts of the world's great faith traditions.
6 x 9, 352 pp, HC, 978-1-59473-264-5 **$29.99**

Spiritual Leaders Who Changed the World
The Essential Handbook to the Past Century of Religion
Edited by Ira Rifkin and the Editors at SkyLight Paths; Foreword by Dr. Robert Coles
An invaluable reference to the most important spiritual leaders of the past 100 years.
6 x 9, 304 pp, 15+ b/w photos, Quality PB, 978-1-59473-241-6 **$18.99**

Spiritual Biography—SkyLight Lives

SkyLight Lives reintroduces the lives and works of key spiritual figures of our time—people who by their teaching or example have challenged our assumptions about spirituality and have caused us to look at it in new ways.

The Life of Evelyn Underhill
An Intimate Portrait of the Groundbreaking Author of Mysticism
by Margaret Cropper; Foreword by Dana Greene
Evelyn Underhill was a passionate writer and teacher who wrote elegantly on mysticism, worship, and devotional life.
6 x 9, 288 pp, 5 b/w photos, Quality PB, 978-1-893361-70-6 **$18.95**

Mahatma Gandhi: His Life and Ideas
by Charles F. Andrews; Foreword by Dr. Arun Gandhi
Examines from a contemporary Christian activist's point of view the religious ideas and political dynamics that influenced the birth of the peaceful resistance movement.
6 x 9, 336 pp, 5 b/w photos, Quality PB, 978-1-893361-89-8 **$18.95**

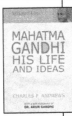

Simone Weil: A Modern Pilgrimage
by Robert Coles
The extraordinary life of the spiritual philosopher who's been called both saint and madwoman.
6 x 9, 208 pp, Quality PB, 978-1-893361-34-8 **$16.95**

Zen Effects: The Life of Alan Watts
by Monica Furlong
Through his widely popular books and lectures, Alan Watts (1915–1973) did more to introduce Eastern philosophy and religion to Western minds than any figure before or since.
6 x 9, 264 pp, Quality PB, 978-1-893361-32-4 **$16.95**

More Spiritual Biography

Bede Griffiths: An Introduction to His Interspiritual Thought
by Wayne Teasdale
The first study of his contemplative experience and thought, exploring the intersection of Hinduism and Christianity.
6 x 9, 288 pp, Quality PB, 978-1-893361-77-5 **$18.95**

The Soul of the Story: Meetings with Remarkable People
by Rabbi David Zeller
Inspiring and entertaining, this compelling collection of spiritual adventures assures us that no spiritual lesson truly learned is ever lost.
6 x 9, 288 pp, HC, 978-1-58023-272-2 **$21.99**
(A book from Jewish Lights, SkyLight Paths' sister imprint)

Prayer / Meditation

Sacred Attention: A Spiritual Practice for Finding God in the Moment
by Margaret D. McGee
Framed on the Christian liturgical year, this inspiring guide explores ways to develop a practice of attention as a means of talking—and listening—to God.
6 x 9, 144 pp, HC, 978-1-59473-232-4 **$19.99**

Women Pray: Voices through the Ages, from Many Faiths, Cultures and Traditions
Edited and with Introductions by Monica Furlong
5 x 7¼, 256 pp, Quality PB, 978-1-59473-071-9 **$15.99**

Women of Color Pray: Voices of Strength, Faith, Healing, Hope and Courage *Edited and with Introductions by Christal M. Jackson*
Through these prayers, poetry, lyrics, meditations and affirmations, you will share in the strong and undeniable connection women of color share with God.
5 x 7¼, 208 pp, Quality PB, 978-1-59473-077-1 **$15.99**

Secrets of Prayer: A Multifaith Guide to Creating Personal Prayer in Your Life *by Nancy Corcoran, csj*
This compelling, multifaith guidebook offers you companionship and encouragement on the journey to a healthy prayer life. 6 x 9, 160 pp, Quality PB, 978-1-59473-215-7 **$16.99**

Prayers to an Evolutionary God
by William Cleary; Afterword by Diarmuid O'Murchu
Inspired by the spiritual and scientific teachings of Diarmuid O'Murchu and Teilhard de Chardin, reveals that religion and science can be combined to create an expanding view of the universe—an evolutionary faith.
6 x 9, 208 pp, HC, 978-1-59473-006-1 **$21.99**

The Art of Public Prayer: Not for Clergy Only   *by Lawrence A. Hoffman*
6 x 9, 288 pp, Quality PB, 978-1-893361-06-5 **$18.99**

A Heart of Stillness: A Complete Guide to Learning the Art of Meditation
by David A. Cooper 5½ x 8½, 272 pp, Quality PB, 978-1-893361-03-4 **$16.95**

Meditation without Gurus: A Guide to the Heart of Practice
by Clark Strand 5½ x 8½, 192 pp, Quality PB, 978-1-893361-93-5 **$16.95**

Praying with Our Hands: 21 Practices of Embodied Prayer from the World's Spiritual Traditions *by Jon M. Sweeney; Photographs by Jennifer J. Wilson; Foreword by Mother Tessa Bielecki; Afterword by Taitetsu Unno, PhD*
8 x 8, 96 pp, 22 duotone photos, Quality PB, 978-1-893361-16-4 **$16.95**

Silence, Simplicity & Solitude: A Complete Guide to Spiritual Retreat at Home
by David A. Cooper 5½ x 8½, 336 pp, Quality PB, 978-1-893361-04-1 **$16.95**

Three Gates to Meditation Practice: A Personal Journey into Sufism, Buddhism, and Judaism   *by David A. Cooper* 5½ x 8½, 240 pp, Quality PB, 978-1-893361-22-5 **$16.95**

Prayer / M. Basil Pennington, OCSO

Finding Grace at the Center, 3rd Ed.: The Beginning of Centering Prayer   *with Thomas Keating, ocso, and Thomas E. Clarke, sj; Foreword by Rev. Cynthia Bourgeault, PhD*
A practical guide to a simple and beautiful form of meditative prayer.
5 x 7¼, 128 pp, Quality PB, 978-1-59473-182-2 **$12.99**

The Monks of Mount Athos: A Western Monk's Extraordinary Spiritual Journey on Eastern Holy Ground   *Foreword by Archimandrite Dionysios*
Explores the landscape, the monastic communities, and the food of Athos.
6 x 9, 256 pp, 10+ b/w drawings, Quality PB, 978-1-893361-78-2 **$18.95**

Psalms: A Spiritual Commentary   *Illustrations by Phillip Ratner*
Reflections on some of the most beloved passages from the Bible's most widely read book.   6 x 9, 176 pp, 24 full-page b/w illus., Quality PB, 978-1-59473-234-8 **$16.99**
HC, 978-1-59473-141-9 **$19.99**

The Song of Songs: A Spiritual Commentary   *Illustrations by Phillip Ratner*
Explore the Bible's most challenging mystical text.
6 x 9, 160 pp, 14 b/w illus., Quality PB, 978-1-59473-235-3 **$16.99**; HC, 978-1-59473-004-7 **$19.99**

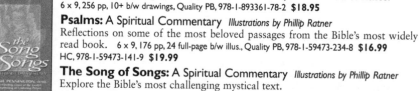

Spirituality of the Seasons

Autumn: A Spiritual Biography of the Season
Edited by Gary Schmidt and Susan M. Felch; Illustrations by Mary Azarian
Rejoice in autumn as a time of preparation and reflection. Includes Wendell Berry, David James Duncan, Robert Frost, A. Bartlett Giamatti, E. B. White, P. D. James, Julian of Norwich, Garret Keizer, Tracy Kidder, Anne Lamott, May Sarton.
6 x 9, 320 pp, 5 b/w illus., Quality PB, 978-1-59473-118-1 **$18.99**

Spring: A Spiritual Biography of the Season
Edited by Gary Schmidt and Susan M. Felch; Illustrations by Mary Azarian
Explore the gentle unfurling of spring and reflect on how nature celebrates rebirth and renewal. Includes Jane Kenyon, Lucy Larcom, Harry Thurston, Nathaniel Hawthorne, Noel Perrin, Annie Dillard, Martha Ballard, Barbara Kingsolver, Dorothy Wordsworth, Donald Hall, David Brill, Lionel Basney, Isak Dinesen, Paul Laurence Dunbar. 6 x 9, 352 pp, 6 b/w illus., Quality PB, 978-1-59473-246-1 **$18.99**

Summer: A Spiritual Biography of the Season
Edited by Gary Schmidt and Susan M. Felch; Illustrations by Barry Moser
"A sumptuous banquet.... These selections lift up an exquisite wholeness found within an everyday sophistication."— ★ *Publishers Weekly* starred review
Includes Anne Lamott, Luci Shaw, Ray Bradbury, Richard Selzer, Thomas Lynch, Walt Whitman, Carl Sandburg, Sherman Alexie, Madeleine L'Engle, Jamaica Kincaid.
6 x 9, 304 pp, 5 b/w illus., Quality PB, 978-1-59473-183-9 **$18.99**
HC, 978-1-59473-083-2 **$21.99**

Winter: A Spiritual Biography of the Season
Edited by Gary Schmidt and Susan M. Felch; Illustrations by Barry Moser
"This outstanding anthology features top-flight nature and spirituality writers on the fierce, inexorable season of winter.... Remarkably lively and warm, despite the icy subject." — ★ *Publishers Weekly* starred review
Includes Will Campbell, Rachel Carson, Annie Dillard, Donald Hall, Ron Hansen, Jane Kenyon, Jamaica Kincaid, Barry Lopez, Kathleen Norris, John Updike, E. B. White.
6 x 9, 288 pp, 6 b/w illus., Deluxe PB w/flaps, 978-1-893361-92-8 **$18.95**

Spirituality / Animal Companions

Blessing the Animals: Prayers and Ceremonies to Celebrate God's Creatures, Wild and Tame *Edited by Lynn L. Caruso*
5¼ x 7¼, 256 pp, Quality PB, 978-1-59473-253-9 **$15.99**; HC, 978-1-59473-145-7 **$19.99**

Remembering My Pet: A Kid's Own Spiritual Workbook for When a Pet Dies
by Nechama Liss-Levinson, PhD, and Rev. Molly Phinney Baskette, MDiv; Foreword by Lynn L. Caruso
8 x 10, 48 pp, 2-color text, HC, 978-1-59473-221-3 **$16.99**

What Animals Can Teach Us about Spirituality: Inspiring Lessons from Wild and Tame Creatures *by Diana L. Guerrero* 6 x 9, 176 pp, Quality PB, 978-1-893361-84-3 **$16.95**

Spirituality—A Week Inside

Come and Sit: A Week Inside Meditation Centers
by Marcia Z. Nelson; Foreword by Wayne Teasdale
6 x 9, 224 pp, b/w photos, Quality PB, 978-1-893361-35-5 **$16.95**

Lighting the Lamp of Wisdom: A Week Inside a Yoga Ashram
by John Ittner; Foreword by Dr. David Frawley
6 x 9, 192 pp, 10+ b/w photos, Quality PB, 978-1-893361-52-2 **$15.95**

Making a Heart for God: A Week Inside a Catholic Monastery
by Dianne Aprile; Foreword by Brother Patrick Hart, OCSO
6 x 9, 224 pp, b/w photos, Quality PB, 978-1-893361-49-2 **$16.95**

Waking Up: A Week Inside a Zen Monastery
by Jack Maguire; Foreword by John Daido Loori, Roshi
6 x 9, 224 pp, b/w photos, Quality PB, 978-1-893361-55-3 **$16.95**; HC, 978-1-893361-13-3 **$21.95**

Spirituality

Claiming Earth as Common Ground: The Ecological Crisis through the Lens of Faith *by Andrea Cohen-Kiener; Foreword by Rev. Sally Bingham*
Inspires us to work across denominational lines in order to fulfill our sacred imperative to care for God's creation. 6 x 9, 192 pp, Quality PB, 978-1-59473-261-4 **$16.99**

The Losses of Our Lives: The Sacred Gifts of Renewal in Everyday Loss
by Dr. Nancy Copeland-Payton
Reframes loss from the perspective that our everyday losses help us learn what we need to handle the major losses. 6 x 9, 176 pp (est), HC, 978-1-59473-271-3 **$19.99**

The Workplace and Spirituality: New Perspectives on Research and Practice *Edited by Dr. Joan Marques, Dr. Satinder Dhiman and Dr. Richard King*
Explores the benefits of workplace spirituality in making work more meaningful and rewarding. 6 x 9, 256 pp, HC, 978-1-59473-260-7 **$29.99**

A Spirituality for Brokenness: Discovering Your Deepest Self in Difficult Times *by Terry Taylor*
Guides you through a compassionate yet highly practical process of facing, accepting, and finally integrating your brokenness into your life—a process that can ultimately bring mending. 6 x 9, 176 pp, Quality PB, 978-1-59473-229-4 **$16.99**

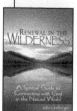

Next to Godliness: Finding the Sacred in Housekeeping
Edited and with Introductions by Alice Peck
Offers new perspectives on how we can reach out for the Divine.
6 x 9, 224 pp, Quality PB, 978-1-59473-214-0 **$19.99**

Bread, Body, Spirit: Finding the Sacred in Food
Edited and with Introductions by Alice Peck
Explores how food feeds our faith. 6 x 9, 224 pp, Quality PB, 978-1-59473-242-3 **$19.99**

Renewal in the Wilderness: A Spiritual Guide to Connecting with God in the Natural World *by John Lionberger*
Reveals the power of experiencing God's presence in many variations of the natural world. 6 x 9, 176 pp, b/w photos, Quality PB, 978-1-59473-219-5 **$16.99**

Honoring Motherhood: Prayers, Ceremonies and Blessings
Edited and with Introductions by Lynn L. Caruso
Journey through the seasons of motherhood. 5 x 7¼, 272 pp, HC, 978-1-59473-239-3 **$19.99**

Soul Fire: Accessing Your Creativity *by Rev. Thomas Ryan, CSP*
Learn to cultivate your creative spirit. 6 x 9, 160 pp, Quality PB, 978-1-59473-243-0 **$16.99**

Money and the Way of Wisdom: Insights from the Book of Proverbs
by Timothy J. Sandoval, PhD 6 x 9, 192 pp, Quality PB, 978-1-59473-245-4 **$16.99**

Creating a Spiritual Retirement: A Guide to the Unseen Possibilities in Our Lives
by Molly Srode 6 x 9, 208 pp, b/w photos, Quality PB, 978-1-59473-050-4 **$14.99**
HC, 978-1-893361-75-1 **$19.95**

Finding Hope: Cultivating God's Gift of a Hopeful Spirit
by Marcia Ford 8 x 8, 200 pp, Quality PB, 978-1-59473-211-9 **$16.99**

Jewish Spirituality: A Brief Introduction for Christians *by Lawrence Kushner*
5½ x 8½, 112 pp, Quality PB, 978-1-58023-150-3 **$12.95** *(A book from Jewish Lights, SkyLight Paths' sister imprint)*

Journeys of Simplicity: Traveling Light with Thomas Merton, Bashō, Edward Abbey, Annie Dillard & Others *by Philip Harnden*
5 x 7¼, 144 pp, Quality PB, 978-1-59473-181-5 **$12.99**; 128 pp, HC, 978-1-893361-76-8 **$16.95**

Keeping Spiritual Balance As We Grow Older: More than 65 Creative Ways to Use Purpose, Prayer, and the Power of Spirit to Build a Meaningful Retirement
by Molly and Bernie Srode 8 x 8, 224 pp, Quality PB, 978-1-59473-042-9 **$16.99**

Spiritually Incorrect: Finding God in All the Wrong Places *by Dan Wakefield; Illus. by Marian DelVecchio* 5½ x 8½, 192 pp, b/w illus., Quality PB, 978-1-59473-137-2 **$15.99**

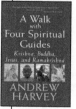

A Walk with Four Spiritual Guides: Krishna, Buddha, Jesus, and Ramakrishna
by Andrew Harvey 5½ x 8½, 192 pp, 10 b/w photos & illus., Quality PB, 978-1-59473-138-9 **$15.99**

Spirituality & Crafts

Beading—The Creative Spirit: Finding Your Sacred Center through the Art of Beadwork *by Rev. Wendy Ellsworth*
Invites you on a spiritual pilgrimage into the kaleidoscope world of glass and color. 7 x 9, 240 pp, 8-page full-color insert, plus b/w photographs and diagrams
Quality PB, 978-1-59473-267-6 **$18.99**

Contemplative Crochet: A Hands-On Guide for Interlocking Faith and Craft *by Cindy Crandall-Frazier; Foreword by Linda Skolnik*
Illuminates the spiritual lessons you can learn through crocheting.
7 x 9, 208 pp, b/w photographs, Quality PB, 978-1-59473-238-6 **$16.99**

The Knitting Way: A Guide to Spiritual Self-Discovery
by Linda Skolnik and Janice MacDaniels Examines how you can explore and strengthen your spiritual life through knitting. 7 x 9, 240 pp, b/w photographs
Quality PB, 978-1-59473-079-5 **$16.99**

The Painting Path: Embodying Spiritual Discovery through Yoga, Brush and Color *by Linda Novick; Foreword by Richard Segalman*
Explores the divine connection you can experience through creativity.
7 x 9, 208 pp, 8-page full-color insert, plus b/w photographs
Quality PB, 978-1-59473-226-3 **$18.99**

The Quilting Path: A Guide to Spiritual Discovery through Fabric, Thread and Kabbalah *by Louise Silk*
Explores how to cultivate personal growth through quilt making.
7 x 9, 192 pp, b/w photographs and illustrations, Quality PB, 978-1-59473-206-5 **$16.99**

The Scrapbooking Journey: A Hands-On Guide to Spiritual Discovery
by Cory Richardson-Lauve; Foreword by Stacy Julian Reveals how this craft can become a practice used to deepen and shape your life.
7 x 9, 176 pp, 8-page full-color insert, plus b/w photographs, Quality PB, 978-1-59473-216-4 **$18.99**

The Soulwork of Clay: A Hands-On Approach to Spirituality
by Marjory Zoet Bankson; Photographs by Peter Bankson
Takes you through the seven-step process of making clay into a pot, drawing parallels at each stage to the process of spiritual growth.
7 x 9, 192 pp, b/w photographs, Quality PB, 978-1-59473-249-2 **$16.99**

Kabbalah / Enneagram
(Books from Jewish Lights Publishing, SkyLight Paths' sister imprint)

God in Your Body: Kabbalah, Mindfulness and Embodied Spiritual Practice
by Jay Michaelson 6 x 9, 288 pp, Quality PB Original, 978-1-58023-304-0 **$18.99**

Cast in God's Image: Discover Your Personality Type Using the Enneagram and Kabbalah
by Rabbi Howard A. Addison 7 x 9, 176 pp, Quality PB, 978-1-58023-124-4 **$16.95**

Ehyeh: A Kabbalah for Tomorrow *by Dr. Arthur Green*
6 x 9, 224 pp, Quality PB, 978-1-58023-213-5 **$16.99**

The Enneagram and Kabbalah, 2nd Edition: Reading Your Soul
by Rabbi Howard A. Addison 6 x 9, 192 pp, Quality PB, 978-1-58023-229-6 **$16.99**

The Gift of Kabbalah: Discovering the Secrets of Heaven, Renewing Your Life on Earth
by Tamar Frankiel, PhD 6 x 9, 256 pp, Quality PB, 978-1-58023-141-1 **$16.95**
HC, 978-1-58023-108-4 **$21.95**

Kabbalah: A Brief Introduction for Christians
by Tamar Frankiel, PhD 5½ x 8½, 176 pp, Quality PB, 978-1-58023-303-3 **$16.99**

Zohar: Annotated & Explained *Translation and Annotation by Dr. Daniel C. Matt*
Foreword by Andrew Harvey 5½ x 8½, 176 pp, Quality PB, 978-1-893361-51-5 **$15.99**
(A book from Jewish Lights, SkyLight Paths' sister imprint)

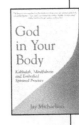

Spiritual Poetry—The Mystic Poets

Experience these mystic poets as you never have before. Each beautiful, compact book includes: a brief introduction to the poet's time and place; a summary of the major themes of the poet's mysticism and religious tradition; essential selections from the poet's most important works; and an appreciative preface by a contemporary spiritual writer.

Hafiz
The Mystic Poets
Preface by Ibrahim Gamard
Hafiz is known throughout the world as Persia's greatest poet, with sales of his poems in Iran today only surpassed by those of the Qur'an itself. His probing and joyful verse speaks to people from all backgrounds who long to taste and feel divine love and experience harmony with all living things.
5 x 7¼, 144 pp, HC, 978-1-59473-009-2 **$16.99**

Hopkins
The Mystic Poets
Preface by Rev. Thomas Ryan, CSP
Gerard Manley Hopkins, Christian mystical poet, is beloved for his use of fresh language and startling metaphors to describe the world around him. Although his verse is lovely, beneath the surface lies a searching soul, wrestling with and yearning for God.
5 x 7¼, 112 pp, HC, 978-1-59473-010-8 **$16.99**

Tagore
The Mystic Poets
Preface by Swami Adiswarananda
Rabindranath Tagore is often considered the "Shakespeare" of modern India. A great mystic, Tagore was the teacher of W. B. Yeats and Robert Frost, the close friend of Albert Einstein and Mahatma Gandhi, and the winner of the Nobel Prize for Literature. This beautiful sampling of Tagore's two most important works, *The Gardener* and *Gitanjali*, offers a glimpse into his spiritual vision that has inspired people around the world.
5 x 7¼, 144 pp, HC, 978-1-59473-008-5 **$16.99**

Whitman
The Mystic Poets
Preface by Gary David Comstock
Walt Whitman was the most innovative and influential poet of the nineteenth century. This beautiful sampling of Whitman's most important poetry from *Leaves of Grass*, and selections from his prose writings, offers a glimpse into the spiritual side of his most radical themes—love for country, love for others, and love of Self.
5 x 7¼, 192 pp, HC, 978-1-59473-041-2 **$16.99**

Journeys of Simplicity
Traveling Light with Thomas Merton, Bashō, Edward Abbey, Annie Dillard & Others
Invites you to consider a more graceful way of traveling through life. Use the included journal pages (in PB only) to help you get started on your own spiritual journey.

by Philip Harnden
5 x 7¼, 144 pp, Quality PB, 978-1-59473-181-5 **$12.99**
128 pp, HC, 978-1-893361-76-8 **$16.95**

Spiritual Practice

Haiku—The Sacred Art: A Spiritual Practice in Three Lines
by Margaret D. McGee Introduces haiku as a simple and effective way of tapping into the sacred moments that permeate everyday living.
5½ x 8½, 192 pp, Quality PB, 978-1-59473-269-0 **$16.99**

Dance—The Sacred Art: The Joy of Movement as a Spiritual Practice
by Cynthia Winton-Henry Invites all of us, regardless of experience, into the possibility of dance/movement as a spiritual practice.
5½ x 8½, 224 pp, Quality PB, 978-1-59473-268-3 **$16.99**

Spiritual Adventures in the Snow: Skiing & Snowboarding as Renewal for Your Soul *by Dr. Marcia McFee and Rev. Karen Foster; Foreword by Paul Arthur* Explores snow sports as tangible experiences of the spiritual essence of our bodies and the earth. 5½ x 8½, 208 pp, Quality PB, 978-1-59473-270-6 **$16.99**

Recovery—The Sacred Art: The Twelve Steps as Spiritual Practice
by Rami Shapiro; Foreword by Joan Borysenko, PhD Uniquely interprets the Twelve Steps of Alcoholics Anonymous to speak to everyone seeking a freer and more God-centered life. 5½ x 8½, 240 pp, Quality PB, 978-1-59473-259-1 **$16.99**

Soul Fire: Accessing Your Creativity *by Rev. Thomas Ryan, CSP*
Shows you how to cultivate your creative spirit as a way to encourage personal growth.
6 x 9, 160 pp, Quality PB, 978-1-59473-243-0 **$16.99**

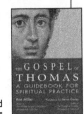

Running—The Sacred Art: Preparing to Practice
by Dr. Warren A. Kay; Foreword by Kristin Armstrong Examines how your daily run can enrich your spiritual life. 5½ x 8½, 160 pp, Quality PB, 978-1-59473-227-0 **$16.99**

Everyday Herbs in Spiritual Life: A Guide to Many Practices
by Michael J. Caduto; Foreword by Rosemary Gladstar
7 x 9, 208 pp, 21 b/w illustrations, Quality PB, 978-1-59473-174-7 **$16.99**

Divining the Body: Reclaim the Holiness of Your Physical Self *by Jan Phillips*
8 x 8, 256 pp, Quality PB, 978-1-59473-080-1 **$16.99**

The Gospel of Thomas: A Guidebook for Spiritual Practice
by Ron Miller; Translations by Stevan Davies 6 x 9, 160 pp, Quality PB, 978-1-59473-047-4 **$14.99**

Hospitality—The Sacred Art: Discovering the Hidden Spiritual Power of Invitation and Welcome *by Rev. Nanette Sawyer; Foreword by Rev. Dirk Ficca*
5½ x 8½, 192 pp, Quality PB, 978-1-59473-228-7 **$16.99**

Labyrinths from the Outside In: Walking to Spiritual Insight—A Beginner's Guide
by Donna Schaper and Carole Ann Camp
6 x 9, 208 pp, b/w illus. and photos, Quality PB, 978-1-893361-18-8 **$16.95**

Practicing the Sacred Art of Listening: A Guide to Enrich Your Relationships and Kindle Your Spiritual Life *by Kay Lindahl* 8 x 8, 176 pp, Quality PB, 978-1-893361-85-0 **$16.95**

The Sacred Art of Bowing: Preparing to Practice
by Andi Young 5½ x 8½, 128 pp, b/w illus., Quality PB, 978-1-893361-82-9 **$14.95**

The Sacred Art of Chant: Preparing to Practice
by Ana Hernández 5½ x 8½, 192 pp, Quality PB, 978-1-59473-036-8 **$15.99**

The Sacred Art of Fasting: Preparing to Practice
by Thomas Ryan, CSP 5½ x 8½, 192 pp, Quality PB, 978-1-59473-078-8 **$15.99**

The Sacred Art of Forgiveness: Forgiving Ourselves and Others through God's Grace
by Marcia Ford 8 x 8, 176 pp, Quality PB, 978-1-59473-175-4 **$16.99**

The Sacred Art of Listening: Forty Reflections for Cultivating a Spiritual Practice
by Kay Lindahl; Illustrations by Amy Schnapper
8 x 8, 160 pp, b/w illus., Quality PB, 978-1-893361-44-7 **$16.99**

The Sacred Art of Lovingkindness: Preparing to Practice
by Rabbi Rami Shapiro; Foreword by Marcia Ford 5½ x 8½, 176 pp, Quality PB, 978-1-59473-151-8 **$16.99**

Sacred Speech: A Practical Guide for Keeping Spirit in Your Speech
by Rev. Donna Schaper 6 x 9, 176 pp, Quality PB, 978-1-59473-068-9 **$15.99**
HC, 978-1-893361-74-4 **$21.95**

Thanking & Blessing—The Sacred Art: Spiritual Vitality through Gratefulness
by Jay Marshall, PhD; Foreword by Philip Gulley 5½ x 8½, 176 pp, Quality PB, 978-1-59473-231-7 **$16.99**

About SKYLIGHT PATHS Publishing

SkyLight Paths Publishing is creating a place where people of different spiritual traditions come together for challenge and inspiration, a place where we can help each other understand the mystery that lies at the heart of our existence.

Through spirituality, our religious beliefs are increasingly becoming a part of our lives—rather than *apart* from our lives. While many of us may be more interested than ever in spiritual growth, we may be less firmly planted in traditional religion. Yet, we do want to deepen our relationship to the sacred, to learn from our own as well as from other faith traditions, and to practice in new ways.

SkyLight Paths sees both believers and seekers as a community that increasingly transcends traditional boundaries of religion and denomination—people wanting to learn from each other, *walking together, finding the way.*

For your information and convenience, at the back of this book we have provided a list of other SkyLight Paths books you might find interesting and useful. They cover the following subjects:

Buddhism / Zen	Global Spiritual	Monasticism
Catholicism	Perspectives	Mysticism
Children's Books	Gnosticism	Poetry
Christianity	Hinduism /	Prayer
Comparative	Vedanta	Religious Etiquette
Religion	Inspiration	Retirement
Current Events	Islam / Sufism	Spiritual Biography
Earth-Based	Judaism	Spiritual Direction
Spirituality	Kabbalah	Spirituality
Enneagram	Meditation	Women's Interest
	Midrash Fiction	Worship

Or phone, fax, mail or e-mail to: SKYLIGHT PATHS Publishing
An imprint of Turner Publishing Company
4507 Charlotte Avenue • Suite 100 • Nashville, TN 37209
Tel: (615) 255-2665 • www.skylightpaths.com
Prices subject to change.